Laurel Highland Legends, Volume I

written by

Marci Lynn McGuinness

Laurel Highland Legends, Volume I

ISBN-13: 978-0938833-51-2

Published in the United States of America by Shore Publications.

www.ohiopyle.info
www.facebook.com/laurelhighlandlegends
www.amazon.com/author/marcimcguinness

Cover Design by Brenda Davis Mihalko, Uniontown, PA

Cover photos:

The Titlow Tavern & Grille, 92 E. Main St., Uniontown, PA. www.titlowtavern.net
The Summit Inn Resort, 101 Skyline Drive, Farmington, PA. www.summitinnresort.com
The Stone House Inn, 3023 National Road, Farmington, PA. www.stonehouseinn.com
Ohiopyle Vacation Rentals, 3054 National Pike, Farmington, PA. www.ohiopylevacationrentals.com
Braddocks Inn, 3261 National Pike, Farmington, PA. Www.braddocksinn.com
Julia Savage and son, Kody, of New Salem, PA, driving Skip Seaton's (Dad & Grandpap) 1915 Apperson Jack Rabbit. Summit Mountain Hill Climb, June 13, 2015

Title Page Photograph: Thomas and Hannah (Holland) Thorpe lived above Ohiopyle on Thorpe Knob and are the author's great, great maternal grandparents. Their property is now a part of Ohiopyle State Park.

DEDICATION

This book is dedicated to all those who share the legends that make the Laurel Highlands of southwestern Pennsylvania unique, and those who have given interviews and donated photographs in order to preserve the region's history.

A special thanks to Jeff D'Miao, Fred Zeigler, Karen Harris, Bill Scott, Ed Cope and Skip Seaton. Their continued support is invaluable to my work.

Ed Cope waited hours to get this shot of a robin feeding its baby. From his back porch in Uniontown, PA, he captured the beauty of the Laurel Highlands in spring time. Photo © Herald Standard.

CONTENTS

ACKNOWLEDGMENTS

I would like to thank God for my writing gift. People often refer to it as a hobby. I smile. Writing is no hobby for me. It is a calling that I can not ignore. Coupled with the intent of preserving legends, I know that I am here to see that our history is not lost, to entertain, and to live a life that is not cut and dried.

In the words of my hero, Ben Franklin:
"If there is one thing writers need to do consistently, it is write, not talk about writing."

Author's Note

Laurel Highland Legends, Volume I is a collection of original stories, photographs, columns, and interviews that depict life in southwestern Pennsylvania. As times continue to change, so much of our heritage gets lost. My hope is that this coffee table book is read by young and old. The old will laugh knowingly; the young will understand a bit more about who they are and where they came from. They will get a glimpse of the non-digital eras that built their world.

Two of my stories, *The Mystery of the Ohiopyle Hotel* and *Vivian & the Board Track Boys*, are historical fiction inspired by true events. I have been privileged to walk these mountains and foothills, to be welcomed into homes and made privy to memories people didn't know they had until they opened up. My hope for this book series is that we can preserve as many stories and photographs as possible of our area. The books will be available on Amazon and on Kindle, and the historical fiction short stories can be purchased on their own, digitally, at: www.ohiopyle.info and www.uniontownspeedway.weebly.com.

Part I of my memoir, *Marci Unblocked*, is also published in this volume for your enjoyment.

Thank you for reading and sharing,
Marci Lynn McGuinness

P.S. In the *Mystery of the Ohiopyle Hotel* story, several names have been changed to protect those involved.

"*If you would not be forgotten as soon as you are dead and rotten, either write things worth reading, or do things worth the writing.*" Ben Franklin

CHAPTER 1

OHIOPYLE AREA LEGENDS

It has been fifty years since someone burnt the beloved Ohiopyle Hotel to the ground. Whodunnit? This is a work of fiction by Marci Lynn McGuinness, inspired by a true story

Mary gazed out the window of the Western Maryland Railroad Station in Ohiopyle, Pennsylvania. The next train wasn't due until 3 a. m. Pen in hand, she listened to the sounds of the night. It was quiet along the Youghiogheny River, except for its constant roar. She pondered her letter listening to the fast moving water, until the Ohiopyle Hotel closed for the night. Men and couples spilled out of the popular tavern there. The Morans provided top notch hospitality. She had had this same trouble in Connellsville, with Lucky's uncles, Ross and Marcus. They owned the hotel by the station there. Made their living selling spirits and entertaining the well to do. "Liquor brings out the devil in men," she said to the night.

Mary had published several stories for New York magazines and a book of poetry, all written at work in the wee hours. After the local World War II soldiers came home, she began a mission she felt was led by God. She was part of the Women's Christian Temperance movement, and used her writing skills to push the town toward her ways.

She listened to the hotel patrons as they walked to their homes across the river bridge or talked beside their cars. Their laughter annoyed her. She dreamed that Ohiopyle would become a show place. She disliked the mountain folk and felt she knew what Ohiopyle should be. She did not have the love a local has for their home. She wanted to stop the men and women from drinking and turn the mountain village surrounding the falls and river over to "civilized" city folk. Although she had a long term affair with a married man during this time, she judged others. Locals wondered how many prayers she said to redeem her soul when her lovers wife killed herself.

Although she did a great thing for the

service men during the war, writing to them, publishing their letters in a church bulletin and keeping them in contact with each other, once they came home she tried to recruit as many as possible to her ways. When they did not follow her as she had dreamed, she took revenge and called it conservation.

Laura and Lucky Moran ran a first rate hotel along the wild Youghiogheny River. She was known far and wide for her homemade bread, noodles, Sunday chicken dinners, orange cookies, and welcoming hospitality. Many of their patrons were from out of state. They came to hunt grouse and pheasant, fish for rainbow and brown trout, sit on the porch swings, and converse with the intelligent Moran family. Lucky and his sons trained bird dogs. He owned property and they took visitors out for a taste of some of the best fowl hunting in the east. The eldest son was an expert fisherman and knew all the mountain streams, every nook and cranny. Fishing parties always ended with Laura frying native trout in her enormous cast iron skillet. Her old cook stove was rarely at ease. For 16 years, the Morans made friends with doctors, lawyers, and the elite. They returned like clockwork, annually, twice a year, some monthly, some every weekend. Life was good for the Morans, but the little lady in the train station was not happy about it. She pretended to be Laura's friend, as she set about on a letter writing mission to shut down the hotel.

She hated the roughness of some of the folks there although she was raised along the railroad and lived in shanties all her life. Her judgment of the locals reeked havoc on them. She especially hated the Bower men, Hunter and the boys. They did chores for the Morans for decades, kept them in eggs and fresh chicken, too. They emptied the burn barrel, found parts to repair plumbing and stoves, plowed the garden, did yard work, and hauled away trash. The sight of them made her skin crawl. When Hunter smiled, showing his tobacco-stained teeth, and nodded hello, hat in hands, she always looked at the ground, scampering away. He would laugh loud and long. “Come on up to the compound some day, Miss. You will never leave,” he told her one day after he heard about the letters she was writing to the Pittsburgh conservationists.

She befriended those who followed her path, no others. Ohiopyle has paid the price of her stern, non-local ways. She did not understand the comradeship and wonderful life they had each carved out of that mountainside, that river, as they raised their children from gardens and fresh game and fish.

Botanists and the like were among the hotel's patrons as Ferncliff Peninsula, (at the hotel's door) holds many rare, southern plants. It also, at that time, held the Ferncliff Hotel, but it closed its doors before Mary's letters found the people she was looking for. The people who would change Ohiopyle from a place of freedom, to a town being slowly bankrupted by a government entity. They took 17 homes and businesses along the falls and, ran off the farming families of Sugar Loaf Mountain and Tharpe Knob, stealing thousands of acres of their land, their homes, “for the good of the people.”

Mary was relentless in her pursuit of a buyer for the hotel and peninsula. Her fear grew as the Morans set out to purchase their beloved home and business from Mr. Meade. Mary was granted her wish when Edgar Kaufmann bought the land and hotel and turned it over to what became the Western Pennsylvania Conservancy. It was 1951.

Lucky passed away in 1955, leaving his widow and sons to run the business and other properties. In the early 1960's, Laura retired. Purchasing the hotel became a dream that was not to come true as the conservancy remodeled it, planing a fabulous grand opening.

The locals were trying to find housing, most had to apply for loans because the stipends they received for their homes and properties was minimal at best. Maurice Goddard was the secretary of the Department of Forests and Waters. They had been receiving Mary's letters for some time. The Ohiopyle falls area was surveyed and the Conservancy went to Goddard seeking assistance to preserve the area for a park.

In 1962, the Conservancy received another plot of land here from the Keister famiy. The deal the Keister family made with them was that the land would be named after them. It is not.

Goddard sold the idea of a state park to the Ohiopyle people promising economic revival, jobs, a resort hotel, golf course, and the like. Many residents wanted to believe as they struggled to stay afloat. Ohiopyle was the number one acquisition in Project 70. Goddard's mission was to preserve several areas for outdoor recreation in the state of Pennsylvania. Money was tight, so eminent domain was enforced on many of the honest working folk. They had to find places to live and work away from their beloved Ohiopyle.

Imagine the anger. It surprises me that no one was killed, but someone came close to murder when a local family took the job as caretaker for the hotel. The state's lawyers were run off at shot gun point many a time, but no one was physically hurt. Then a Conservancy worker was threatened.

The next day was Friday, November 13, 1964. A drought had gripped the area for two months. The wind was brisk over the fast moving white water river. A couple families lived in the cabins on the hotel property. The Watson family, just hired as caretakers, was in the hotel.

As darkness fell, someone came out of the woods behind the hotel on the north side. They walked up the steps and onto the porch at the kitchen door. They stacked dry kindling wood and newspapers against the hotel and lit it afire with a silver engraved cigarette lighter. They walked slowly away, through the woods, and up the hill across Route 381. They sat and watched as Mrs. Watson screamed from the upper floor. Tippy, the King family dog, barked, waking Till who went out on his cabin porch to see what was amiss. He heard the screams then, saw flames and went running.

He found a ladder nearby as the hotel was still having finishing touches done before the grand opening. He slammed it against the hotel and climbed without thinking. His wife, Jeanie, called the firemen. By the time they arrived from several townships, the Watsons had been rescued and the hotel was burning to the ground. The drought and wind assisted a human's hand and one small flame in destroying the historical landmark.

Hunter and the boys were on the hillside watching the fire. They walked around the property and came to the building across the street. Hunter knocked on the door as firemen hosed down the apartment building to keep it from catching on fire. Laura Moran answered. Hunter had his hat in his hand. He nodded his head and said, "I am sorry,

Ma'am. I wanted to be sure you were unharmed."

She handed him a bag of homemade rolls and a jar of orange marmalade. "It is a sad night," she frowned, waving good night to the men.

The detective on the scene was about to retire, and he did, quite promptly. His files for the case were never reviewed as no one was "really hurt" and the next detective to take his desk moved on to other matters. With what had been going on in Ohiopyle, the local cops knew they did not want to deal with the state government or the locals. So they didn't.

Buildings and homes were taken down and removed to clear the area around the falls for tourists, while those who had invested their lives to their land and homes were shuffled off, victims of Project 70.

The locals were heartbroken over the loss of the hotel and meeting place, but not about the loss for the conservancy. People speculated about the culprit, but the locals did not care. They felt the conservancy deserved what they got, at the very least. Was someone trying to hurt the Watsons for accepting the care-taking job? Everyone in town was questioned, but no one was talking. And the Morans were so enthusiastic about future prospects in tourism, the law felt they had no real suspects, but many suspects at the same time.

Fifty years later, Detective Aspirin, a distant relative of the Watsons, became intrigued with the cold case. He opened the slim file. One man's name jumped out at him. He recognized it. The man was a legend. Godfather of Ohiopyle, so to speak. He was not to be crossed, but what did this mean? His name had a ? next to it. Did he know who did it? Did he do it? Have it done? He had motive and opportunity, but so did several hundred others. Detective Aspirin always had a hunch about who did it, since he was a kid hearing the story from his elders. It was time to test that hunch, he knew.

Nothing was left to check out as far as new DNA was concerned. There was no evidence, but he could interview the survivors. It was Spring Buckwheat Supper weekend in the Ohiopyle borough, so he went up for lunch that Friday afternoon in 2015.

He wore his jeans and fleece jacket, no suit for this mission. He wanted people to see him as one of them, not a detective on the job. No one knew he had taken this on, not even the Captain. It was best to just sniff around a bit to see if there was anything there to investigate after all.

Climbing Summit Mountain that sunny day, he took several deep breaths as he passed by the Summit Hotel. He knew he should have brought his partner, but he was not going into a crack house or after a killer. It was just buckwheats. But is it ever really just buckwheats in a small town? He found a parking place along the top side of the play ground on Grant Street. Children played in the "Green", given to the town by Congressman Andrew Stewart before the Civil War. While paying his fee for the dinner ticket, someone slapped him on the back.

"My God, is it the law?" an old woman asked.

"Hi, Aunt Grace," he said. "Are you alone?"

"Well, I am not on a date," she cackled. "Why are you here?"

He paid for her ticket, too. "I am starved," he said, leading her to the table the hostess pointed out. It was too busy for conversation. Several people came to ask if they wanted things like buckwheats or pancakes, home fries, sausage, apple sauce, gravy and the like. The service could not be topped. He was grateful as he did not want to have a conversation with Aunt Grace at that time. The place was noisy, bustling. The food came fast and they ate heartily while he watched the locals and travelers enter and leave.

"You are up to something. I can tell," Aunt Grace announced.

"Right now I need to take a walk." He patted his stomach and smiled. A lady friend came over to Grace and took her away to a neighboring table of friends. He sighed thankfully, smiled, left a couple of ones on the table and attempted to find his way into the adjoining shops.

A line formed at the wine room in Backyard Gardens. He enjoyed this store of local goods in the old school house. Wine, pepper mustard, local books, honey, old fashioned wooden toys, paintings, photographs, fresh produce, cheeses, soaps, candles, handmade jewelry and even locally roasted coffee were available for sale. He had some coffee, purchased the stores own jalapeno mustard and chatted with the owner, Vicki. She told him that she was very small when the hotel burned, but there were photos in one of the *Yesteryear in Ohiopyle* books her cousin published. He bought the set of three volumes and an *Explorer's Guide*. With about 700 photographs between them, he thought they could help direct him to folks who may have bits of information.

But first, he took a drive about two miles north on Route 381, turned right onto a dirt road, turned the car around and parked outside the gate where Frank Bower lived. This was Hunter's son. He remembered the last time he was there, when Frankie's pregnant sister lost her life in a burning shed. He shivered although it was 75 degrees. Snarling, growling, barking, indescribably vicious canines slammed themselves against the gate trying to get to him. He was unsure if any of the other brothers were still there or even alive, until he blew the horn. Several long haired, dirty, loping men came out of buses and out buildings. One man, Frankie, opened the front door holding a shot gun. He smiled a toothless, filthy grin at the detective and proceeded to the gate. The others followed. Barbed wire topped the fence of the junk yard. He looked the scene over and grinned at Frankie when he stopped and leered at him.

"Got a warrant?" he said and spit tobacco on the ground.

"Nope. I don't want in," he assured him.

"You get in, you don't get out," Frankie stared at him, laughing.

"That's what they say," he said. "You know if your Pap burnt down the Ohiopyle Hotel when you were a kid?

"F... you."

"Did he or didn't he? You can't get in any trouble, unless you lit the match that started the fire."

"I 'member the fire. Big, quick. The screamin'. Was walkin' home with Pap. We emptied ashes and such 'cross the street for the ladies that night."

"You sure he didn't go over to the hotel and set a fire on the porch?"

Frankie shook his head. "Pap was workin'. You sure you don't want in?" The dogs were still very loud, and aggressive.

"Thanks," he said and waved goodbye. Frankie laughed and shot the gun in the air. His brothers laughed, too, tipping a jug.

He was thirsty, a little shaken, and wanted

to relax with a beer. He pulled into the Ohiopyle Cafe and took a seat at the downstairs bar. The owner, Stacey, greeted him and set him up with a beer. "You look familiar," she said.

"I am a detective," he whispered.

"Are you on duty? Looking for someone?"

"Off duty," he said and raised his glass. "Cheers." He drank and she waited on the young river guides at the other side of the bar.

"I am looking for someone but don't know who yet," he confessed when she returned. "Know anything about the Ohiopyle Hotel burning way back. You wouldn't have been alive, but I am looking into that fire."

"No way!" she laughed. "Why?"

"The case was never solved. That bothers me. The Watsons are relatives of mine."

"There were people sleeping nearby in cabins and the apartment house across 381, but I think it burnt too fast for anyone to see who started it."

"That is what is in the report. No evidence."

She shrugged her shoulders. "My great grandparents ran it before that."

"You are a Moran?"

She pointed at a sign that said, "Welcome to Moranville." They both laughed.

"Was Bob your grandfather?"

"Yes, why do you know that?"

"My father knew him well. They were in the service together. He had great respect for him."

She smiled and went to take care of the rest of her customers. He chatted with a woman who was Stacey's cousin. She told him that she remembered the the fire well. She said that she could not remember any talk about who did it at all. No one had apparently known that the Watsons were going to be there that night, she claimed. People just figured it was payback from the locals. End of story.

He smiled. "Maybe that is all there is to it, but that still doesn't tell us who lit the match."

"Nope," she said, turning her back to him.

An old man walked in the door, around the bar, and sat on the last stool at the edge of the bar where Stacey stood when she had a chance to stop for a moment. "Uncle Phil," she said before hugging him.

He was only a stool away from the Detective and he leaned toward him and whispered, "You LCB? You look like it."

"No."

"You sure?"

"Positive." He showed Phil his badge.

"Detective, huh? Who you after?"

"You," Stacey laughed while walking away from them to get Phil a beer.

"She's kidding, in a way," he said.

"What does that mean?" Phil eyed him suspiciously.

"Where were you when the hotel burned down in 1964?"

"Home with my wife. Where were you?"

Detective Aspirin laughed. "I am just looking into this cold case to see if I can figure out who started the fire back then. The Watsons are family."

"Oh," was all Phil said. He got up and moved to the other side of the bar.

"What did you say to him?" Stacey asked when she returned to see if he wanted another beer.

"I am not making friends, I can see that."

"No one wants trouble," she said and walked away again. She went to Phil and they had a quiet talk. Detective Aspirin stood, left a tip, and walked out into the late afternoon sunshine. He walked across the Youghiogheny River bridge and stood staring at what used to be the spot where the hotel sat. It was filled in with dirt in the 1960's when they cut the sharp curve out of Route 381. He turned and looked at the ever-flowing river from that perspective, climbed the embankment and looked out as if he was on an upper floor of the hotel. He closed his eyes, pictured the hotel, the back porch, someone sneaking up there with newspapers and matches. He opened them suddenly and jumped when the train whistle blew.

"That must have woke up folks at the hotel," he said out loud to himself. He climbed down and crossed the street to the Falls City Pub. A crowd was gathered outside at the picnic tables and on the large boulders. The train still chugged by, a long one, blocking the view of the river for several minutes. He walked up to the bar checking out the boats and whatnot on the walls and ceiling. He took a seat around the far end of the bar where he could watch and observe with his back to the wall, and ordered a water and a beer.

An old man showed up about halfway through that beer and sat a stool down from him. "You're in my seat," he said.

"Do you want it? It's a good one."

"No, no. I am alright," he smiled.

They sat in silence and watched the white water community intermingle. The old man said, "Not a bad view here, huh?" referring to the young women.

He smiled and bought the old man a drink.

"Got a name?"

"Woodson," he said.

"A local, I take it?"

"Yeah, you are from Uniontown aren't you? A cop?"

"I guess I am not so stealth."

"Looking for someone? Drinking on the job?"

"Neither."

"Bullshit," he laughed.

They sat in silence and watched the growing crowd.

"Were you around when the Ohiopyle Hotel burnt in '64?" the detective asked.

"I knew there was something on your mind. Yes, why?"

"Wondering who set the fire is all."

"Is all?" Woodson laughed heartily. "That's stirring the pot, if you ask me."

"What is the big secret? Did a local do it and everyone has covered all these years?"

"You already have it figured out, what are you doing here?"

"Do I?"

"Hell, no," Woodson said, finishing his beer. "Want a shot?" he asked Detective Aspirin.

"Patron on the rocks, salted rim, lime," he told the river rat bartender in his tie dyed shirt.

They toasted to the old hotel.

"What's your interest?" Woodson asked.

"Watsons are distant relatives. Wondered if someone was after them."

"Huh."

"Look, I know what the state did to the locals in this town. I understand the heartache and resentment toward anyone who would work for them, especially back then. I just want to know what actually happened."

"Why? What are you going to do with the information when you make your big discovery?"

"I guess it depends what the information

turns out to be. I am not officially on this case. It is cold and hasn't been reopened."

"Got it."

They ordered another round.

"It was a helluva watering hole," Woodson mused. "Anyone who ever had Laura's fried chicken and noodles, returned the next Sunday for more. It was awful, what happened to the place. It shoulda never been sold to Kaufmann if that is what he was going to do with it. They lied. Said everyone would still have their jobs. The government always lies."

"Hard to keep that promise when the place burnt, though," the detective pointed out.

"You just don't know."

"Clue me in, then."

The detective ordered another shot for each of them. The place was packed with river guides and bicyclists.

"Meade shoulda sold to the Morans like he always promised. He got greedy."

"Musta made the Morans good and mad."

"Them and a couple hundred others. It was the last straw."

"So, who lit the match?"

"Not who you think, I am sure of that," he laughed loud. Several tourists looked their way.

"Who do I think?"

"It was no man."

"What are you sayin'?"

"You're the detective. There, I gave you a clue. Do what you will with it."

Woodson stood and walked out of the bar.

"A woman?" he said in a whisper."

"That seat taken?" a young lady asked. He finished his beer and followed Woodson outside. "Hey, hey, Woodson. She still alive?"

He sat down at the last picnic table and Detective Aspirin joined him. "You want something to eat, Harry?" the waitress asked Woodson.

"The usual," he smiled. "You hungry?" he asked Aspirin. "Make it two of the usual, honey."

"So, I realize there were dozens of people angry enough to strike back, but who was crazy enough?"

"Please understand that I will not be naming any names."

They laughed halfheartedly together and ate the black bean burritos put before them. People and dogs came and went.

"If it was someone working for the state, one of the locals would have proved it by now," he said to Woodson with a mouthful of avocado.

"Mountain people have their own ways."

"So, it was a local, then. Had to be."

Woodson looked across the road toward the old hotel. "People were angry for many reasons. There's another hint." Woodson paid his tab and stood. "Good luck, Detective," he said.

Aspirin watched him go. He had an idea and mulled it over while walking back across the river bridge, watching the flow from the middle "Yough" above the waterfall. He smiled and nodded to passersby, strolled to the Ohiopyle Falls, the reason the park came to be. He breathed in the ions offered by as the water flowed into the gorge of rapids. He gazed across the falls and its boulders to Ferncliff Peninsula with its rare plants. "No wonder they wanted to preserve this. Who wouldn't want to own it. Those poor people didn't have a chance once the ball got rolling," he said a bit louder than he realized. A couple looked at him and smiled. He nodded.

That night he read through all the Ohiopyle books one by one. He took several legal pads full of notes and began highlighting the most important information.

He started a document on the laptop with all of the characters involved. Their motives, their locations at the time. What each person had said to him that day. He realized Woodson was right. It could have been so many people, but it was one person. Who?

The Morans wanted to buy the hotel. Many families were mistreated and had their properties stolen from them to make way for the park. Businesses and homes were torn down.

"I can see why they gave up back then," he mumbled to himself. "You really can't blame the locals for striking back. Burning the hotel was a huge message, but the Watsons were in there, making it much more than arson due to pay back. God, I am always talking to myself. I should get a dog."

He pulled the old files again and went over them. "Mad is one thing, taking action is another," he thought. Then there it was. The loose end he was seeking. A shoe was found just up the embankment. A rather new woman's shoe, sturdy, size 8. It did not belong to the Watsons and it had not been there long. Some may think that a lady was angry. That after all the work she had done to get the conservationists to preserve Ferncliff and the falls area, things were backfiring. They were going to continue serving alcohol, something she could not allow.

"Maybe she wanted folks to assume the Morans had the Bowers do it," he said aloud. "Great plan. Makes sense." Or it could be one of the ladies who owned a home or business or farm. Or it could be nothing, just a shoe. Maybe we will never know, he thought.

He went to the evidence room as soon as he could to find the shoe. He went through all the Ohiopyle books again. There were many school and church group photographs from long ago. All the people involved were there. He looked at everyone's feet until he found a match.

Should he share his findings? There was no way of really knowing positively. He could be quite wrong. It was just a shoe in the woods.

The borough of Ohiopyle was a village where hundreds lived well, before the park took over. Today, a handful of people live in the borough of Ohiopyle, struggling to keep the park from taking their town. Help save Ohiopyle. Join their Spirit of the River fundraiser, May 21, 2016.

OHIOPYLE'S HISTORY

OHIOPYLE MEANS "WHITE FROTHY WATER OR BEAUTIFUL FALLS" IN THE LOCAL INDIAN LANGUAGE (SHAWNEE).

YOUGHIOGHENY MEANS "RIVER RUNNING IN A ROUNDABOUT COURSE" IN THE LOCAL INDIAN LANGUAGE.

Ohiopyle, Pennsylvania remains one of the country's wonderful hideaways. The gem of Pennsylvania's state park system has been through many changes as has the borough of Ohiopyle, in order to accommodate visitors and grow with the times. As this process has taken place, I have been snapping photographs so that the town's history is at least partially recorded. In *Yesteryear in Ohiopyle,* Volumes I and II, I depicted Ohiopyle and area folk, buildings and scenes of many years ago. *Yesteryear in Ohiopyle,* Volume III is a record of the 1990's destruction of Castle Rock, Meadow Run Cabin, the Meadow Run Bridge, the old Western Maryland Railroad bridge and the reconstruction of local bridges and buildings. If you have the first two volumes of *Yesteryear in Ohiopyle*, you will want to add the third volume to your collection to keep a consistent log of Ohiopyle's history through the decades.

In my book, *The Explorer's Guide to the Youghiogheny River, Ohiopyle & S.W. Pennsylvania's Villages,* published in 2000, I wrote a more complete history on Ohiopyle (1600 – 2000) than was included in the earlier books. It begins with details of George Washington's travels through the area, his stopping above the falls and refusing to take his canoe over the rushing water, and Congressman Andrew Stewart's development of Falls City here.

Ohiopyle had its heyday at the turn of the century with four hotels, and the Baltimore & Ohio railroad bringing passengers from Cumberland and Pittsburgh to lounge along our gorgeous river. These days are covered in the history taking you through the depression when Edgar Kaufmann bought the Bear Run property where he had Frank Lloyd Wright build the famous Fallingwater. Kaufmann also purchased Ferncliff Peninsula the Ohiopyle Hotel and granted them to the Western Pennsylvania Conservancy and virtually propelling us to where Ohiopyle is today.

I feel the need to insure that the changes in this unique town and park are set down in history so that future residents and visitors have a record of the local people and Ohiopyle during this particular era of our high energy but slow keyed mountain river town.

What makes the Youghiogheny River so special? Below the falls it drops 90 feet in the first two miles and 13 feet per mile for the next five miles. There are 22 White Water rapids in 7 1/2 miles within the Youghiogheny River gorge. But I would say, beyond the obvious thrill of the wild ride down the river, it is the negative ions that get you. They make people feel invigorated, and the Youghiogheny oozes with them. Two million people pass through this fair burgh every summer season. They come to ride the river, stand by the falls and soak up the ions, eat ice cream and take walks on the many trails, ride on the Yough bike trail, swim, picnic, and relax by the river. Ohiopyle continues to make people feel good even after they return home.

Stewart Township was named after the Honorable Andrew Stewart in 1855, because the Congressman put his money where his heart was in the early days of Falls City (Ohiopyle). He bought up thousands of acres in the mountains, but it was the lush Ferncliff Peninsula that intrigued him! After a detrimental flub by the Whig nomination chairman cost Stewart the office of Vice President of the United States, President Taylor paid a visit to Uniontown. He arrived at the Clinton House Hotel on February 21, 1849 where hundreds gathered to greet him. Andrew Stewart built the Clinton House and lived there for many years before it was turned into a hotel. Was it here that the President offered Stewart the office of Secretary of the Treasury and was turned down? I have no information to confirm this yet, but I have a hunch that is why he made the trip to Uniontown. Taylor soon died and Fillmore took the Presidency as Stewart should have. But our Andrew stayed busy. During the remaining twenty three years of his life he kept in tune with Washington and worked very hard to bring the B & O railroad through Falls City (Ohiopyle). In addition to his business interests, he owned part of the Madison College in Uniontown and was President of the board. When they turned it into the Soldier's Orphan School during the Civil War, he set up $10,000. worth of annual scholarships for hard working students. This went on until his death although the school was moved to Jumonville.

In 1862, Stewart replaced the covered bridge over the Youghiogheny River in Ohiopyle with a tall steel model. The ends of the covered bridge were steel and were hauled up to Cucumber Run. Here a bridge over the creek was built. This bridge was replaced in 1999/2000. As he served as President of the region's committee to bring the railroad to the area, he also drew up plans for Falls City's future. In 1868 a maintenance building was erected here for the railroad workers. What an exciting time for Falls City residents and the Stewarts! By now he was an elderly man, but his energy continued. His sons David, Albert and Col. Andrew worked with him, helping to run his vast estate. In 1871 the railroad came through Falls City and the Stewarts turned a huge barn into the three-story Ohiopyle Hotel. It sat on the immediate north side of the B&O train station here. A general store was also opened in the hotel building. Stewart was ready for the flow of traffic and industry the railroad would bring. This
same year Stewart built the wooden Meadow Run Bridge, making Falls City more accessible.

On July 16, 1872 the Honorable Andrew Stewart passed away and left his family his vast holdings referred to as the Stewart Estate. He was eighty two years old, a long life at that time. I believe that after he succeeded in bringing the railroad here, he was able to relax knowing his sons would carry on with his plans to make Falls City a travel destination of recognition. After the estate was settled, his widow sold Stewart's Row in Uniontown and the Fayette Springs Hotel (Stone House) on the National Road.

By 1879, the Stewarts built the four story

Ferncliff Hotel on the 100 acre Ferncliff Peninsula. It was the picture of glamor with running water throughout boasting eight hundred electric lights, and the best in cuisine and service. An archway bearing its name led travelers from the B&O station down a long boardwalk. "Our porters meet all trains" was part of their ad then. The boardwalk led up to the hotel on the hill and down to the river where a bathhouse, bowling alley, and pavilion were built for the enjoyment of patrons. "Western Pennsylvania's Outing Resort" had a dining room that sat 150, hot and cold baths with iron and sulfur water, tennis courts, a baseball diamond, fishing, bathing, and picnicking. There were reading and reclining chairs throughout the woods in addition to a croquet court, many swings, and refreshment tents. The Ferncliff Hotel overlooked the Ohiopyle Falls and the Cucumber
Falls and Meadow Run Slides were within close walking distance. The town of Falls City could be seen from Lover's Leap, an overlook on the Ferncliff side of the falls. The Spoke and Hub Works, Fayette Tannery, Planning, Grist & Saw Mills, Thomas Potter's Coal Mine, and the Falls City Shook Factory could be viewed from above. Wooden steps led down the cliff to the falls where visitors could enjoy the river. Surrounded by water, the peninsula offered both a relaxing and energetic atmosphere with all the modern conveniences of the great hotel. Other than a few small cabins, the hotel was the only building ever constructed on the Ferncliff Peninsula.

The Coal and Coke Boom was underway and the Youghiogheny River Gorge, mined and timbered. Throughout the next decade, stores, liveries, and businesses were erected and the population grew to eight hundred-the most who have ever resided here! In 1891, Falls City's name was changed to Ohiopyle and the town was incorporated in to a borough. Ohiopyle means beautiful falls and white frothy water in the local Indian tongue. This same year a law was imposed carrying a fine of $5.00 - $25.00 for swearing or taking the Lord's name in vain.

At the turn of the century Ohiopyle boasted four hotels: The Ferncliff Hotel, the Ohiopyle House, Dr. Brady's Boarding House, and the Ranier Hotel. Passenger trains brought travelers from far and wide keeping the hotels over booked. Many residents and farmers rented extra rooms to weekend guests and times were good. This time, from the moment the railroad came to town in 1871, to the great depression of the 1930's, were six decades of prosperity. In 1903 the Stewarts tore down and rebuilt the Ohiopyle Hotel. Both their hotels were thriving and they had been building houses and stores in Ohiopyle and selling them and selling lots. I have yet to find out why they never built the subdivision their father had son Albert design. His son, Colonel Andrew Stewart died in 1903. With William dying heroically at sea, Fannie
losing her life as a baby, Elizabeth passing in 1894, and David Shriver Stewart in 1897, Albert was the only child of the Congressman left to carry on his estate. Albert lived until 1916. The Stewarts had owned two hundred acres here-the entire town and the peninsula. Most of the buildings and houses were built by them. They gave the town the "Green" where the playground area is and the land where the fire hall sits. This was originally given to the Presbyterian Church but the church has long been gone.

The Brady Boarding House burnt down in 1916 along with Tom Flemming's Store and several homes. These were located across the Youghiogheny from the town and across the street from the Ohiopyle Hotel. Men doused the hotel with water and saved it. The Downer Excursion House also burned this year. In 1903 Tim Mitchell and his crew were cutting timber off of Ferncliff. They built a swinging bridge to get the logs across the river. Cable track was laid on the bridge and horses hauled wagon loads of lumber across the river! Since this is the year the Ohiopyle Hotel was rebuilt and son Col. Andrew died, I assume they were clearing land for their 337 lot village. I don't yet know why Albert never went on with things. I do know he did no building on the peninsula after his last brother died. All the Stewart's Ohiopyle property was sold off through the years.

The Ohiopyle Lumber Company opened in 1905 which became the Kendall (Samuel and Jacob) Lumber Company in 1915. They built a 26 mile narrow gauge tram road from Meadow Run to West Virginia to haul logs. They logged four thousand acres south and east of Sugarloaf Mountain. They worked this mill on Meadow Run into the early 1920's. The wooden Meadow Run Bridge was replaced in 1919 with the one that was recently replaced. By the late1920's many owned automobiles (which had a hard time climbing mountains) and the tourist trade fell off. The 1930's brought the great depression and times became hard here in Ohiopyle. The Ferncliff hotel was abandoned and the 1936 Johnstown Flood destroyed the Big Gristmill at the falls. Even the jailhouse and meat packers were washed away. Many moved away to find work. Moonshine stills and Speak Easies became the norm because mountain spring water was plentiful...and the Youghiogheny River kept flowing on. My mother grew up in Ohiopyle in the 1930's and 1940's and tells me she never noticed that it was hard times here. They were perfectly happy and ate well.

From Moonshine to Mainstream...

Helen Hochstetler Snyder, who graduated with the Ohiopyle Class of 1938, wrote the following poem about that era:

Ohiopyle Memories

by Helen Hochstetler Snyder

As I grew up in Ohiopyle in post-depression days,
I heard many tales of what it was like when Ohiopyle was in its "hey-day".
How excursions came from Pittsburgh where city folks did dwell
How they spent their summer holidays at the grand Ferncliff Hotel
There was a boardwalk, so they said, winding through the park
And how I wished I could have been there. It would have been a lark!
The good old "Yough" was our playground and every spring we'd shiver,
Trying to be first to take a dip in that sparkling, flowing river.
Things have changed, and once again,
Ohiopyle's the place where people come from far and near and down the rapids race
My childhood home is standing still and memories abound
When I go back to Ohiopyle it's the greatest place around!

In 1906 the Kendall Lumber Company harnessed the water power at the Ohiopyle Falls to produce electricity. They not only ran their saw mill and plant, but the lights of the town as well. Residents will tell you, that when the river froze over in the winter, lights would dim and finally go out until someone went down to the freezing Youghiogheny and broke the ice up. Folks argued about whose turn it was, for the weather was atrocious and no one was anxious to go out to the roaring ice-laden Yough. The depression hit and many businesses failed. The Ferncliff Hotel ran through the late thirties and was abandoned, but the Ohiopyle Hotel continued it's rein through 1964.

Just three miles away, in 1936-38, Edgar J. Kaufman (Kaufman's Department Stores)was building the now famed Falling Water. Kaufman employed many locals in the construction of his new Frank Lloyd Wright masterpiece. He ran a full time greenhouse and dairy farm on the acreage and some of his main workers lived in cottages there. Many saw mills and mines were still in business, but not in the capacity that they had produced during the coal and coke boom. Some men were hired to build the Youghiogheny River Dam and the Pennsylvania Turnpike, but many turned to moonshining and running speak-easies to make a living.

Lillian McCahn worked at the Western Maryland Railroad Station in Ohiopyle for 25 years. This station was built in 1911 by the river where the Baptist Church once sat. It is today's visitor's center. In 1948 McCahan wrote to the Western Pennsylvania Conservancy asking them to buy the Ferncliff Peninsula to save it as a natural area. She knew of the rare southern plants and wanted to see it used as a park for picnicking. The conservancy did not have the funds to buy the 100 acre Youghiogheny paradise. Three years later she was in a panic as then owner Alex Meade wanted to sell the peninsula for $35,000. His prospective buyer intended to build an amusement park. She contacted Dr. William Mayer-Oakes, a Carnegie Museum anthropologist whom she had met in Ohiopyle, and he agreed that this was an important piece of property to conserve. He discussed the situation with M. Graham Netting of the Recreation, Conservation, and Park Council. Along with Charles Lewis from the conservancy, they approached Edgar J. Kaufmann. In 1951 he bought the Ferncliff Peninsula and the Ohiopyle Hotel from Alex Meade for $40,000. He then turned them over to the conservancy, unaware that he had just made the first move toward what would become Ohiopyle State Park, white water haven.

Around 1910, Ohiopyle residents began adding bathrooms to their houses. Up until that time, everyone used outhouses. The sewage ran through open ditches down the alleys to drains that took it right into the river. Most people had chickens and some say Ohiopyle smelled real bad between the sewage and the chicken do-do. At this time high school students took the train to Connellsville for their education.

The Conservancy Cometh

Down close to the river along the falls area, there was a road called Front Street or Commercial Street. Stores, homes, and blacksmith shops lined this lane.

In 1958 the conservancy announced its intention to preserve the Youghiogheny River Gorge from logging and mining. The Melon Trust Fund awarded the conservancy $100,000. to plan and develop a park in Ohiopyle, and to acquire land. They hired Community Planning Services in 1959 to analyze the land here and recommend boundaries for their dream park. The Youghiogheny River Gorge and all river front property became a priority. Borders extended upriver to Ram Cat where the Laurel Hill starts and south to Bruner Run. Sugarloaf Mountain's north slope was included because of the wonderful slopes for skiing, along with Baughman Rock's scenic overlook. Tharpe Knob ridge on Kentuck Mountain was included for camping, a possible golf course, overlooks, and Jonathan Run. Meadow Run, with its natural rock water slides and falls went into the plan, also. That same year, the West Penn Power Company gave the conservancy its riverfront property that ran from the Route 381 bridge to Meadow Run. In 1960 they announced that they would build a parking lot, trail, and picnic area at the Ohiopyle Falls.

In 1961, Mrs. Albert Fraser Keister sold 589 acres to the conservancy including one mile of Cucumber Run, the Cucumber Falls, and two miles of river frontage. Mrs Keister did this with the stipulation that the park be called "Keister Park" and for a while it was, but when the land was sold to the state for a state park, this promise was not kept. It was around this time that the conservancy and the state agreed that all the land here that the conservancy acquired would be sold to the state at cost.

Maurice Goddard was appointed Secretary of the Department of Forests and Waters in the 1950's. Frederick L. Olmstead, Jr., surveyed the state's recreation needs and recommended that Ohiopyle be designated as a park. So, when Charles F. Lewis approached Goddard promoting the Ohiopyle area for conservation, he listened.

In 1962, at the dedication of the Keister acquisitions (now totaling 1,000 acres), Goddard announced his dream to "create a full scale state park here at Ohiopyle-one which will be almost unmatched in natural scenic beauty anywhere in Pennsylvania." To acquire more land, Goddard began Project 70 with the goal of opening an 18,500 acre park here by 1970. Ironically, $70 million dollars were allocated in 1963 to buy lands in Ohiopyle for a major state park. Goddard led the team that condemned the property belonging to Ohiopyle residents to make their park. He said he hated to condemn land but was doing it for the common good. This created hard feelings between the state park, conservancy, and the locals that still exists today. Homeowners began getting letters saying, "Your home will be bought."

They were no longer asking to purchase, they forced the people who loved their homes to sell at rock bottom prices. Most could not afford another place and had to move in with relatives or buy a much more modest home. Fights ensued, but the government won.

On Friday, November 13, 1964, just after the Ohiopyle Hotel was remodeled by the conservancy, someone burnt it down. The fire was started on the porch during a severe drought. It seemed to be a local's way of saying, "You may get our land, but you will never take our hotel." The hotel and tavern was first built in 1871. My grandmother ran the place until 1963. Seventeen homes and buildings were destroyed along the area where the falls overlook and park were created. The Ferncliff Hotel was also torn down and burnt, but you can see its remains still on the Ferncliff Peninsula.

In 1958, Lance Martin ran the Youghiogheny River's rapids as an Explorer Scout in an Army surplus raft. Five years later, he, wife Lee, and friend Karl Kruger began taking people down the lower Youghiogheny for money. This marked the birth of the biggest white water rafting Mecca in the world.

In 1968, 5,000 people were taken on guided tours down the river. This figure rose to 95,000 for the season of 1978 and to 150,000 by1982. Lance pioneered Wilderness Voyageurs, one of four guided rafting companies in Ohiopyle today. Now his children run the business and are proud of what their father did for this borough.

In the late 1960's Route 381 was rerouted and Front Street removed. Sewage and water plants were built for the borough bringing city water and stopping the continual pollution of the Yough. This was one of the ways the conservancy tried to ease the local's anger, but the people who were run from their homes no longer lived in the borough and could not benefit.

Holt's General Store was the center of social activity (today's Fall's Market). Thomas and John Holt were brothers who brought their families here from Pittsburgh for the clean air. Thomas was ailing from black lung disease. In 1895 John built a store by the bridge along Front Street. This did so well that in 1918-19 he constructed the large brick store . At that time the store was downstairs and Dodges and Chevys were sold upstairs. In later years Bob and Charles Holt opened stores next to each other. They were not on good terms and never set foot in one anothers stores! Charlie's son Bill later bought the store and ran it for decades until selling to Leo and Sally Smith in 1975. They ran the gathering place for 31 years.

Falls Market is the corner of Ohiopyle that everyone recognizes, and the store has been remodeled and upgraded over the past decade with outdoor seating. Locals still greet you and cook your meals, making a kind of history of their own in the landmark establishment.

Fifty Years of Youghiogheny River Rats

Lance Martin came to Ohiopyle with his Boy Scout troop to run the Youghiogheny River rapids, and never looked back. Half a century ago he and wife, Lee, started a business that would propel Ohiopyle, Pennsylvania into white water fame. Today, his family still runs Wilderness Voyageurs, offering trips on several rivers, rock climbing and over night adventures.

Four companies run rafting trips in Ohiopyle and this has drawn thousands of river guides to the borough through the decades. In my 1999 book, the *Explorer's guide to the Youghiogheny River/Ohiopyle*, I interviewed then veteran river guides, Eric Martin, Bobby "Needle" Daniels, Donnie Hasch and Bo Harshyne, of Booville.

The one and only (late) Donald 'Bo' Harshyne has left us with this advice, "Remember the Golden Rule of white water rafting. NEVER panic and try to stand up. Foot entrapment is the most dangerous part of the trip."

Bo says, "There are two kinds of rocks. Big ones and little ones. The little ones will stop you. Shift your weight away from the rock. Big ones will flip you upside down or pin you. DO NOT PANIC OR STAND. Get your feet up and float to a calm pool at the side of the river.

Bo worked for Laurel Highland River Tours for many years and ended his river career at the Ohiopyle Trading Post. We were friends, but the first time I met him, he grabbed me from behind and spun me around. I punched him between the eyes.

The next day my Uncle Phil Marietta stopped at our home on 132 Grant Street in Ohiopyle. He was laughing when I opened the door. "You know you gave Bo two black eyes," he smiled.

A couple hours later Bo knocked at the door. He apologized and gave me a little bow from the waist. We were friends for life after that.

Through the past 50 years thousands of "river rats" have come to work on the Youghiogheny. Some stay before they go.

Bo Harshyne left us June 2, 2014. There was only one Bo. He spent 32 years guiding the Yough, Cheat, Gauley and Russell Fork Rivers, but more importantly, he was a local character. He stayed in "Booville" in an Airstream trailer summers.

There was no one like him and never will be. Bo put down his paddle, but I bet he is WOW WOWing wherever he is. Ohiopyle thanks you for your time and dedication, Bo. WOW WOW, WOW WOW! *Photo donated by Felipe Glover.*

©Kevin O'Brien

A Paddle Crafting Legend...
Keith Backlund, paddle master. Keith was a character and friend who went out hard. If you are lucky enough to own one of his paddles, treasure it. He put his talent and love into it. Photograph (Confluence, 1982) by the legendary Kevin O'Brien.

Backlund

A Tribute to Haze Marietta McGuinness,

Bob, Haze and Phil Marietta, Ohioplye, 1945. Haze takes her last swim in the Youghiogheny.

River Rat Extraordinaire, 1929 - 2015

Hazel Laverne Marietta McGuinness grew up in Ohiopyle, Pennsylvania in the house that is now a part of the White Water Adventurers Outfitters buildings. She ran the T Shirt Shop there for many years for her brother, Bob. Haze is well known in the old guide crowd and shared many an ice cream with them on the bench in front of the store.

Mom was the youngest child of four for six years until brother Phil came along. She was the type of kid who never got into trouble, and became a lady many respected. When she swam, she did so with grace, never getting a hair on her head wet, never splashing. She swam with a smile.

Haze grew up with many cousins, namely, the Corristan sisters, Charlotte, Nancy, Beverly and Roberta. Her neighbors, Donna Ruth Hall Rose and Wanda Burnworth Lineberry were lifelong friends. Through more than five decades, this group of ladies, in addition to her sister, Maralee, gathered for lunch every Thursday. Many times they went go to a play or to Phipps Plaza for a flower show.

Mom did not date much, but met her husband, Richard "Muggs" Thomas McGuinness at the Connellsville A & P Store where they both worked. They had ten babies together and raised nine of them, with Jonathan Fitzgerald dying as an infant.

In the year 2000, Mom wrote a few passages in a journal. I quote her here:

"My mother named me after Aunt Hazel. Everyone called me "Hazy" when I was a kid and many people in Ohiopyle still do. I shared a bedroom with my sister Maralee. I thought it was a large room, but now I know that it was very small. We had lots of toys, dolls, dishes, books, etc. And one thing I remember is we each had a small iron stove like the old fashioned cooking stove fired with coal. The lid

would lift off and doors opened in the front. We also had Shirley Temple dolls and Little Orphan Annie sweaters.

Our bedroom overlooked Mr. Wildey's blacksmith shop. We would go down and watch him shoe horses. He would heat the horse shoes in the forge and pound them to fit on the anvil. Also, when we opened our bedroom window, you could hear the falls.

We went to Sunday School on Sunday morning and sometimes to church on Sunday evening. In the summer we went to Bible School for two weeks. On Christmas Eve we were always in a program and we sang and recited verses, and had Jesus' birth in the manger.

When we went home, we were allowed to open one package that would be from our parents. It would be gloves or a scarf.

In season on Sunday, they would have ball games in the park. We went for many hikes in the park and played on the swings and see saws there. We also roller skated, played hide and seek and kick the can. We played with dolls, went sled riding, built snow men, and went for walks, taking a sandwich for a picnic. We swam, read and listened to the radio. I played with Wanda Burnworth, Charlotte Corristan, Donna Ruth Hall, Sara Lou Cunningham and Gertie Thorpe.

When I was young, my dad worked in timber. He had a saw mill and a very large work horse which we were allowed to ride sometimes. When we went to the saw mill, we were allowed to jump in the saw dust. When my brothers (Bob and Jim) got older, they went to work with him to cut logs. During World War II my brothers went to the Army and Dad drove a pony in the coal mine because he couldn't get any help to run the saw mill during the war. After I was older, my dad and mother ran the Ohiopyle Hotel.

When I was young, my Mom cleaned the house and washed clothes by hand on a wash board after she boiled them on a coal stove. Then she ironed them with an iron that was heated on the coal stove. She made a lot of our clothes. Also, she planted the garden, took care of it, and canned a lot of the vegetables for the winter.

Charlotte Said What?

The following photograph of Charlotte Corristan Fosbrink shows her in her later years on the porch of her home-place in Ohiopyle. Charlotte was Mom's cousin and playmate. She became the mother of four, wife to Charles "Fuzzy" Fosbrink, and a fabulous friend and grandmother. Her granddaughter, Emily, was kind enough to send me a few of the one-liners she was known for. We love you, Charlotte...

"You are drunker than Cooty Brown!"
"Even a blind squirrel finds a nut once in a while."
"That stuff will make you throw rocks at your own car."
"You are batting your eyes like a frog in a hail storm!"

Charlotte Corristan Fosbrink, Ohiopyle native and one funny gal, left us this year.

Joey Marietta and Laura Bell Morrison Marietta, Mom's Mom. This is her garden on Grant Street in the 1970's. I made the dress "Nanny" is wearing. Her arthritis forced her to enlist my sewing skills for many years.

Mom and Dad operated the Ohiopyle Hotel together until his death. This was from 1947 – 1955. Then she and my brothers operated the hotel until about 1961. After that she worked at the Ohiopyle School cafeteria until she retired.

My mother taught me my first prayer and it was, "Now I lay me down to sleep, I pray the Lord my soul to keep. If I should die before I wake, I pray the Lord my soul to take."

Our living room had wall paper but I can not remember the color. The furniture was called overstuffed, and we had carpet on the floor. The other rooms had linoleum on the floor.

I can remember when we got our first radio and phonograph. The radio was a floor model and the phonograph you cranked by hand.

I loved living on Negley Street in Ohiopyle. You knew everyone and everyone knew you. The 'Green' has always been the place to play and all the kids gathered there. In the evening we played games until dark. When you were a little older, you could go to the river or the park or take a hike in the woods. No one worried as long as you were home at meal time.

Grandma and Grand-pap Morrison were my only living grandparents. They were wonderful. They lived in different places, usually in the woods where there were very few houses. We visited them often, and were allowed to go and spend a week or more with them in the summer. They had chickens and a few other animals and lots of room to play.

They taught me to play cards and every night after supper, as soon as the dishes were done, they played cards until bed time. Grand-pap Morrison worked in the woods and was killed when a tree fell on him. This happened when I was in grade school, then Grandma moved to Ohiopyle.

Ed Jackson, Ohiopyle WWII Vet

Some people tell a story so well, they mesmerize you. This happened a few years ago when I visited Ed Jackson, 89, of Ohiopyle. His tales were so compelling, I knew I would go back when we could record his life story. He would be 90 that June. On a Sunday I joined his family to record his tales. He had planted black walnut trees and grape vines with daughter, Tammy, earlier that day. I knew when I met him that he was not an average man.

Ed's father was Barton Jackson of Ohiopyle. When he was 18, he went to Reedsville, to work in the Steel Mills where he lost his leg. Bart came home and worked on his uncle's farm on Kentuck Mountain. He saved his money, buying himself an artificial leg. He had a 6" stump while working on the farm, mind you. He was paid $8. per month by the mill until he bought the leg, then they felt he was fit to work and stopped paying him. It was the early 1920's.

He had other pressing matters on his mind, namely, Alice in Reedsville. Bart could not read or write, so his sister wrote the love letter that brought Alice to the mountains. They married. "I can remember playing with your uncles, Jim and Bob. We lived next to them on Jim Run when we were 3 and 4 years old. Our mothers were friends."

When I asked if he remembered the depression he said, "I do recall the day Dad came home and said he had no job. The timber outfit he worked for shut down. Mom cried."

Dad said, "We have this farm. It's not much but we can grow food." And they did.

Ed worked on the farm as a kid. He was nine years old when they cleared the nearby plot for Kentuck Church. He had a strong horse named King, who Elmer Wallace hooked to a large oak tree. Ed knew the tree was way too big. "Make him go," Wallace ordered.

"I kicked King in the ribs. The harness broke and I went rolling out over the yard. No bones were broke."

"Get on that horse!" Wallace yelled as he pitched the young Jackson up on King.

Stories like this make me realize how Norman Rockwell-like my childhood was. Ed remembers helping his father pour the cement for the church basement. It was cold so Bart had them build barrel fires to dry the floor. They stayed up the entire cold autumn night. "We put corn fodder around the outside, too, to keep it warm."

He then drove a horse team logging in the woods at 13 years old for his uncle. He was "paid" room, board and 50 cents. "You got fed, but no money. They used it for coal. I lived close-by so I didn't need boarding." Ed was unimpressed with that deal so he went to work logging for my grandfather, Buck Marietta.

Ed started working full time after 8th grade. He, Rob Taylor and Buck dragged trees in to the saw mill below Kentuck Church. Tug (Morrison) and Jim and Bob (Marietta) worked the mill. One day when Rob arrived back for lunch, the men had eaten everything from his bucket, filling it with horse poo. They then tied it to a sapling. He had to cut the tree, which threw his bucket. The hungry

Taylor also got to wash his bucket out.

"Besides that, when did you have fun?" I had to ask.

"We had two swimming holes. That's where we bathed. On Saturday nights we went to Ohiopyle to a show."

Before WWII Ed worked in a coal mine near Smithfield. His natural engineering aptitude had his boss trying to keep him from going oversees. He did go, for 35 months. Here he was trained as a Specialist Engineer to place runways behind enemy lines.

Ed's life ingenuity is evident in his beautiful five bedroom home, which he built at 68 years old, without designs, by hand. He tapped his temple, "I had it all up here."

Ralph Morrison, Ed and Ethel (Thompson) Jackson on their wedding day in 1957, Beulah Thompson.

Ed and Ethel Jackson fifty years later, 2007!

Lillian's Sewage Mystery

Ross Rogalski sent me this note after reading my story, *Mystery of the Ohiopyle Hotel.*

When Lillian McCahan sold her home at Sherman and Sheridan to Mom and Dad, they continued to let her rent it for awhile, until she could retire from the Western Maryland RR. We vacationed there briefly late one summer, I think it was August 1969. That fall, Wanda and Bobby Lineberry, Jr. stayed there with Aunt Sadie while Bob, Sr. did a tour of duty overseas. I remember something about them being relieved that he was not assigned to a combat unit in Vietnam. Bobby Jr. attended Ohiopyle Elementary that school year.

Wanda was concerned because the drains never seemed to run quite right. When she drained the kitchen sink, soap bubbles came up in the yard.

When Wanda and Bobby were reunited with Bob, Sr. and followed him to his next assignment in the Air Force, dad started digging to find the leak / blockage. He spent the summer digging, starting at the kitchen sink, all the way around the house to the front of the house where the drain from the two sides joined together, and then finally, out to the street. It was out along the street that the drain plunged deep. Dad dug down at least six or seven feet deep, and finally found the problem. The drain was simply not connected to the sewer line!

He paid a professional plumber to make the connection, and at last the drains then ran properly. It took us most of the next summer to back-fill the holes and ditches.

Nobody else seemed to have had a problem not being connected to the sewer. It had been a long standing mystery in our family why / how the line had never been connected. So many people stopped by to watch dad dig that trench and holes...someone had to know.

When we got the holes filled in, dad build a ramp at the corner of the porch were the stairs used to be. Pretty sure I saw it was still there when we drove by this past December. The corner concrete pour has our hand prints in it and the date...August 1972? ...if I'm remembering right. There also used to be a rock on the corner next to the maple tree. Dad found that buried down close to where the sewer line wasn't connected. He "engineered" it up out of the hole using a stack of Aunt Sadies kindling wood. First, he got a wedge under it, then he tipped the rock toward the wedge and put a piece of kindling wood under it. Then he tilted it to one side or the other and kept building up the kindling wood under the rock until he "walked" it up high enough so he could roll it out of the hole. The things my dad used to do "for fun"!

Don't suppose someone added that rock down there just to make digging the sewer line out "an extra treat"?

Still...in all, Lillian would have been what 60+ in 1964 ... when the hotel burned? It's a little bit of a stretch to imagine a "senior" getting involved in something like that? Still...it was Ohiopyle...and folks like Aunt Sadie were carrying firewood and working their gardens well into their 90's? So, maybe 60 was like "old enough to know better ... but young enough to still want to..."

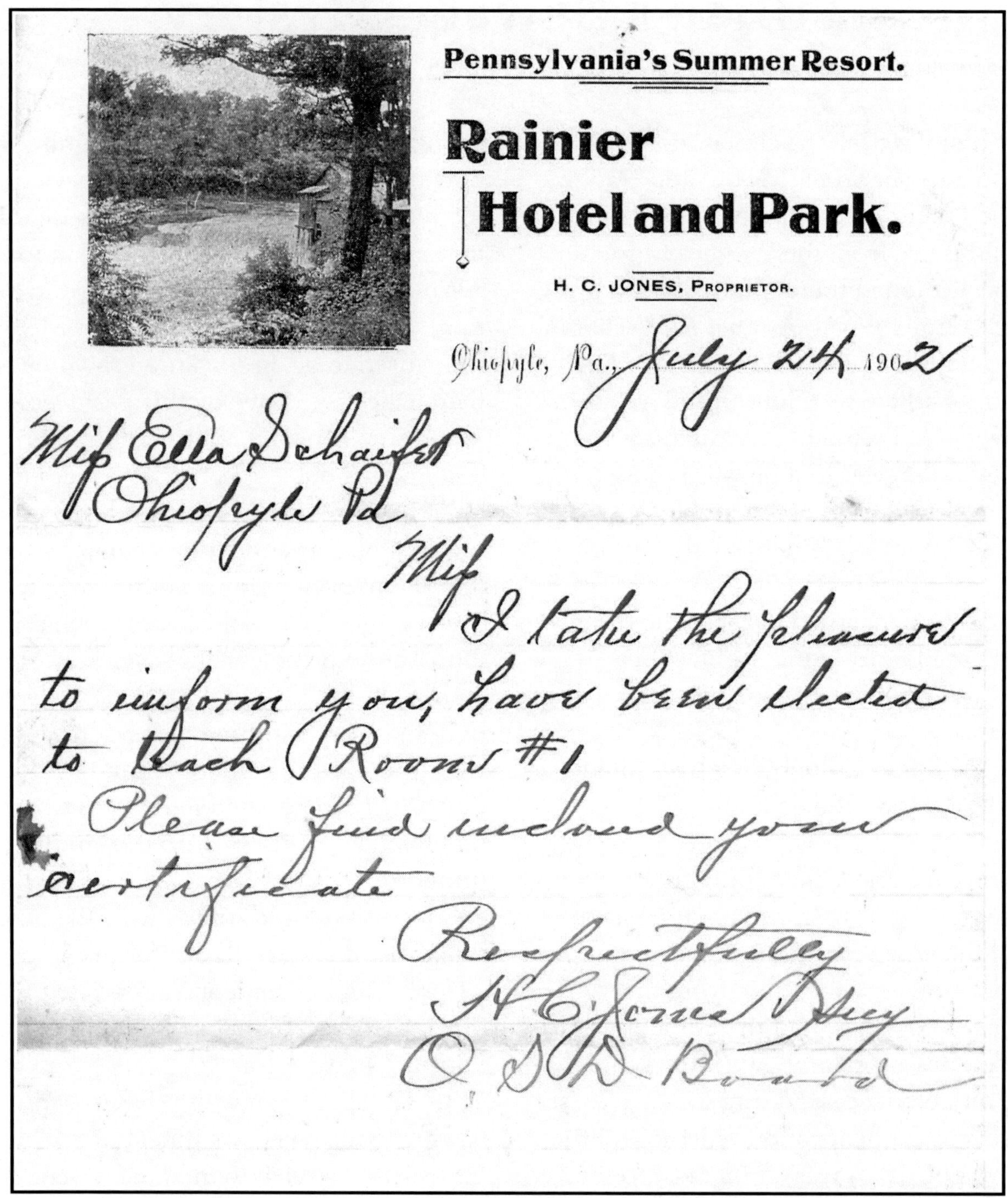

Pennsylvania's Summer Resort.

Rainier
Hotel and Park.

H. C. JONES, PROPRIETOR.

Ohiopyle, Pa., July 24 1902

Miss Ella Schaifer
Ohiopyle Pa

Miss
I take the pleasure to inform you, have been elected to teach Room #1
Please find enclosed your certificate

Respectfully
H C Jones Secy
O S D Board

In the early 1900's there were three hotels in Ohiopyle, the Ohiopyle House Hotel, Ferncliff Hotel and the Ranier. This is a letter and envelope that was sent on Ranier Hotel stationary to Ella Schaifer in 1902, letting her know she had been elected to teach Room #1 at the Ohiopyle School.

Can you identify the children in this 1956 Ohiopyle School photograph?

Remains Of Ohiopyle Hall After Blaze

—Evening Standard Photo

The ruins pictured above are all that remain of the Ohiopyle I. O. O. F. Hall, destroyed in a $20,000 fire Sunday night. Four fire departments battled the flames, which evidently started after the building was struck by lightning. The hall was used as a meeting place by several organizations and offices of Dr. E. E. Phillips were on the first floor.

In 1984, the University of Pittsburgh Press published the book, *Youghiogheny,* Appalachian River, by Tim Palmer. On November 10, 2012, I ran into Tim on an airplane, giving us a chance to chat from Chicago to Pittsburgh. It has been 30 years since he did the research for his still popular book. I thought it would be interesting to take a look at some of the historical changes in Ohiopyle, since then.

Ohiopyle State Park has partitioned off a large part of the Falls area for their new offices and visitor's center. This is not news or a surprise, but it got me thinking about all the buildings and landmarks removed since the *Youghiogheny* book hit the stands. One in particular was a youth hostel.

Tilghman "Tim" Mitchell's house sat on the west side of Route 381 just after you cross the bridge from the borough and over the railroad tracks. He and wife, Cora (Jackson), built the "rambling Victorian" in 1916. He was a well-to-do lumber man during the coal and coke boom. Tim Palmer interviewed Mitchell's son, Shelby, and published the following quote in his book.

"The Mitchell house at Ferncliff was a local mansion, testament to the wealth that could be taken from the old Appalachian forest. Shelby counts the rooms: 'Three in the attic, then seven upstairs, then downstairs there was one, two, three, and the kitchen, breakfast nook, the big billiard room and downstairs, and the wine cellar. Altogether I guess there were about twenty two. A stuffed deer head hung over one of the three fireplaces, and young Ed Jackson was afraid to go in that room.'"

Shelby built a twelve room home during the depression after a fire took the Victorian. He sold the house and property to the Western Pennsylvania Conservancy in 1961. The Pittsburgh Council of American Youth Hostels promptly remodeled it to sleep 22 overnight visitors.

I had written about the hostel in my *Explorer's Guide* after interviewing Manager, Bob Utz, in 1999. It was then an American Youth Hostel with 25 beds, a laundry, television, VCR, outdoor Bar B Q, and a kitchen stocked with everything from bread pans to spices. The common areas and dining room were comfortable and inviting. In their guest book I found an entry declaring that Utz should get an award for the most helpful, friendly hostel manager in the United States. *Hostels U.S.A.* rated them an "Extreme Value" with an A+ in hospitality and cleanliness. Beds started at $9.00 per night and a couple private rooms were available. Only a few years later, I returned for a visit when I was living on the Chesapeake Bay, and it was gone.

I remembered the first time I saw the adjacent plot without the Ohiopyle Hotel. I was nine years old and in shock. Visitors today will never see Castle Rock, the Meadow Run Cabin, the Ohiopyle Hotel, the Hostel, the old bridge with its rope swing, Hostetler's Store, Front Street, or the homes of the many interesting characters who chose to settle near the Ohiopyle Falls. I remain thankful for having them embedded in my memory.

The old stone Ohiopyle schoolhouse one block east of the falls, is still standing and being put to good use. In addition to holding yoga classes, bingo, and spring and fall buckwheat suppers, it is home to Backyard Gardens, Oddly Enough (two unique shops), a pizza joint, and a History Room. Backyard Gardens is a Buy Local store supporting locally produced products from pepper mustard to soap.

Tim Palmer's *Youghiogheny*, Appalachian River, is available at: www.timpalmer.org. He has written 22 books on rivers, the environment, and adventure travel. One of the last sentences in his "Ohiopyle, The Old Days" chapter goes, "I think of changes coming to Ohiopyle and to everyplace, and it seems that there should be some connection between the old and the new." I guess that is where I fit in.

Phil Marietta celebrated his 80th birthday July 14, 2015. He is the last of Buck and Laura Marietta's children, having lost his sister, Haze, in March of this year. Jim, Bob and Maralee preceded them. At his surprise party in the Ohiopyle School-turned-Community Center, I took a few photos. Here, Jim Dean, Phil Marietta, Charlie Bigam and Ed Daniels barely stand still for this, that is why it is fuzzy. I had to move Charlie physically into the shot and ask Ed to stop chewing. Love them all. :) 7-12-15

Speaking of Charlie Bigam, he gave me a photo of Hickman Chapel years ago.

1934...Hickman Chapel Church

It is located on Route 381 just north of Ohiopyle. Notice the small cemetery behind the church.

Ohiopyle Vacation Rentals

Venture to the mountains year round. Relax in style or hold a wedding. OVR is your destination.

www.ohiopylevacationrentals.com

Choose from historic homes, cabins, cottages, and retreats. OVR is your getaway. **877 574-STAY**.

Stone House Inn, Est. 1822

The Stone House Inn at 3023 National Pike, Farmington, Pennsylvania has been owned by several characters, including Congressman Andrew Stewart, George Titlow, Fannie Ross and Rhonda and Fred Zeigler. The Zeiglers are now headed into their 20 year anniversary (summer 2016). Under their ownership, the business has flourished in a different way than the popular Italian restaurant of the Fannie Ross era.

Today they offer original and modern rooms, some with hot tubs. They hold Thursday bike nights and have a popular BBQ pit drawing hundreds to their vast parking area. The restaurant is full most any time they open their doors, year round, and their reputation is that of a fun place to be. When I asked Fred Zeigler about his vision for their future, he said, "I want people to have fun in our mountains." Not a bad plan, I'd say.

Congressman Andrew Stewart

Haunts Stone House 143 years

George Titlow (standing on right side of steps) bought the Fayette Springs Hotel in Farmington in 1909. Congressman Andrew Stewart had built it almost 100 years prior to this photo. Titlow added the front stone addition and named it his Stone House. In this photograph, the Congressman, who passed away in 1872, watches the Fayette County Bar Association (which he was a member of for decades) as they pose for the camera. He stands in tuxedo and top hat in the second window from the left above the porch roof.

Stone House staff and patrons will tell you many stories of seeing the Congressman wandering the halls...and walking into the same room on the second floor most every day. He had been laid out here at the time of his death and still wears his best tux. Have you seen the Congressman? Senator William Crow, who lived across the National Road, stands on the porch third man from the left.

BRADDOCK'S INN REVITALIZED

The year 2015 marks a revitalization of the much loved Braddock's Inn at 3261 National Pike, Farmington, Pennsylvania. Here it is under construction (left). The grand opening in 2015 marks a new era. Looking good!

Braddocks has long been known for their buckwheat cakes and seasonal flea markets. Rhonda and Fred Zeigler have remodeled the building to allow for more fun, and are already holding events on the property along our historical National Pike.

Braddocks is named after the general who came here and lost his life while causing hundreds of fatalities and casualties fighting in a war the Englishman was not prepared for. Mountain man,Tom Fossit, shot him and George Washington buried him in the road near Fort Necessity. Fifty years later, Fossit showed road workers where to find the General. His remains were moved here, next to Braddocks Inn, where he rests today. www.braddocksinn.com

THE HISTORIC SUMMIT INN RESORT, EST. 1907

WHERE GUESTS STILL MEET LIKE YESTERDAY'S ELITE

The Summit Hotel on top of Summit Mountain was headquarters for the Uniontown Hill Climbs, 1913 – 1915. Here, a crowd of 4,000 await the start of the races.

It sits high atop Summit Mountain, a landmark for millions of travelers. They used to come by carriage, then automobiles began arriving. The Historic Summit Inn was built by a group of businessmen in 1907, just one year after the Titlow Hotel opened in Uniontown. The Honorable J. C. Work, Issac W. Semans, Frank H. Rosboro, B. B. Howell, Dr. Charles H. Smith, John F. Hankins, John M. Core, M. H. Bowman all of Uniontown, and W. W. Ramsey of Pittsburgh formed the Summit Hotel Company, opening the doors of a remarkable enterprise.

It was the coal and coke boom era. Uniontown was home to dozens of millionaires. The rich and famous filled the Summit Hotel's rooms and veranda overlooking Uniontown. They were quite modern, boasting, "Ample telegraph and long distance telephone facilities."

GUESS WHO SLEPT AT THE SUMMIT INN!?

All over America you see signs, "George Washington slept here." Recently, owner, Karen Harris, allowed me to delve into their old guest books. We knew that Henry Ford and friends stayed there, but many other famous characters were quite at home in the hotel on top of Chestnut Ridge.

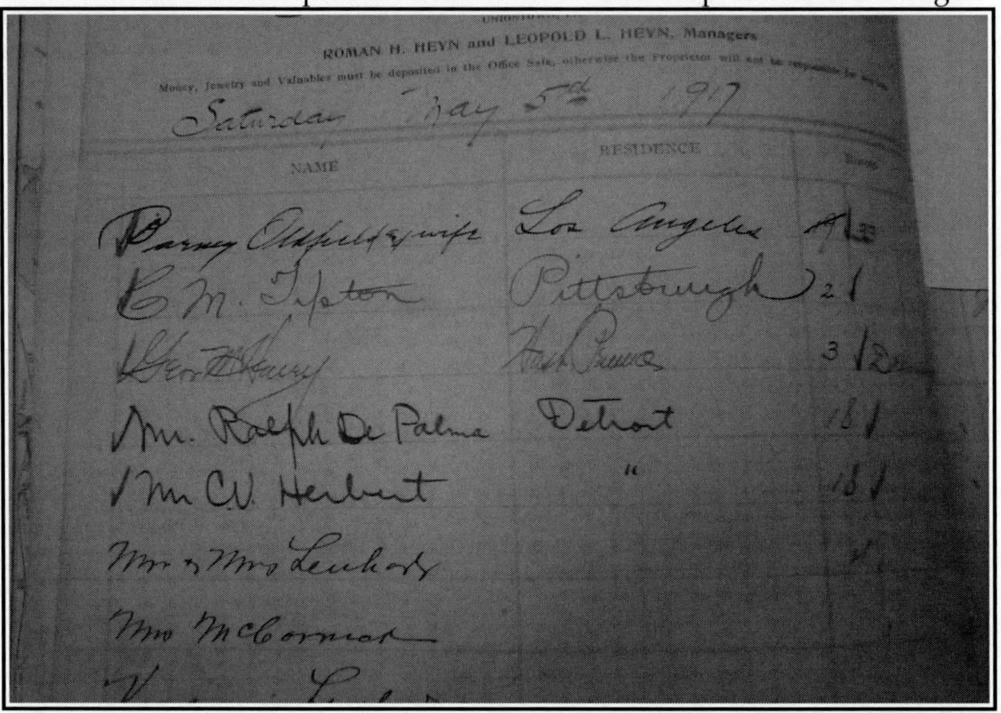

To prepare for the grand opening race at the new Uniontown Speedway board track in 1917, Barney Oldfield and wife, and Indianapolis 500 champ, Ralph DePalma, slept here.

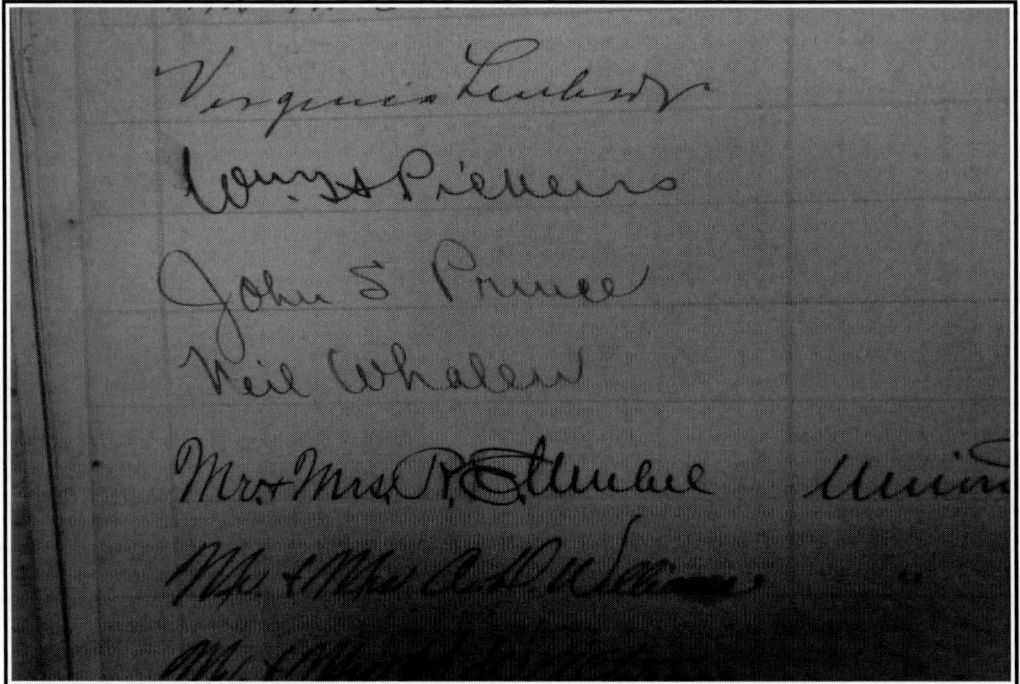

John S. Prince slept here after designing the famous Uniontown Speedway board track. Neil Whalen slept here often. He was flagman, promoter and manager of events and was married to silent film star, Vivian Prescott.

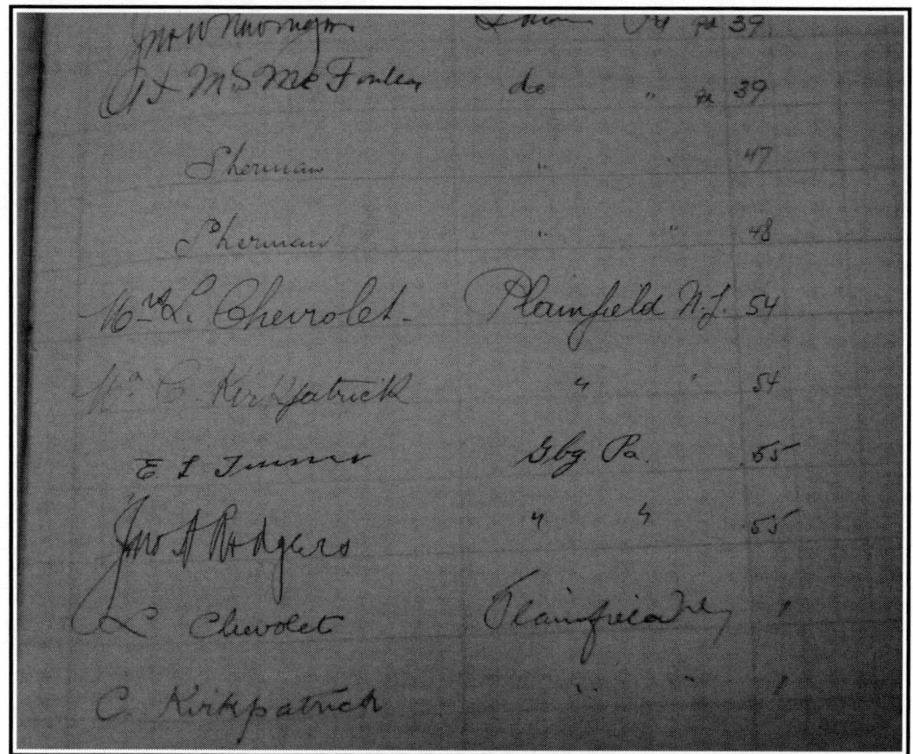

Sherman	" "	47
Sherman	" "	48
Mrs L. Chevrolet	Plainfield N.J.	54
E L Turner	Gbg Pa.	55
Jno A Rodgers	" "	55
L Chevrolet	Plainfield N.J.	1
C Kirkpatrick	" "	1

Louis Chevrolet checked into room #1 while his Misses took room #54. Louis had won the Universal Film Trophy in the big race just five months earlier, when five men lost their lives at the new track.

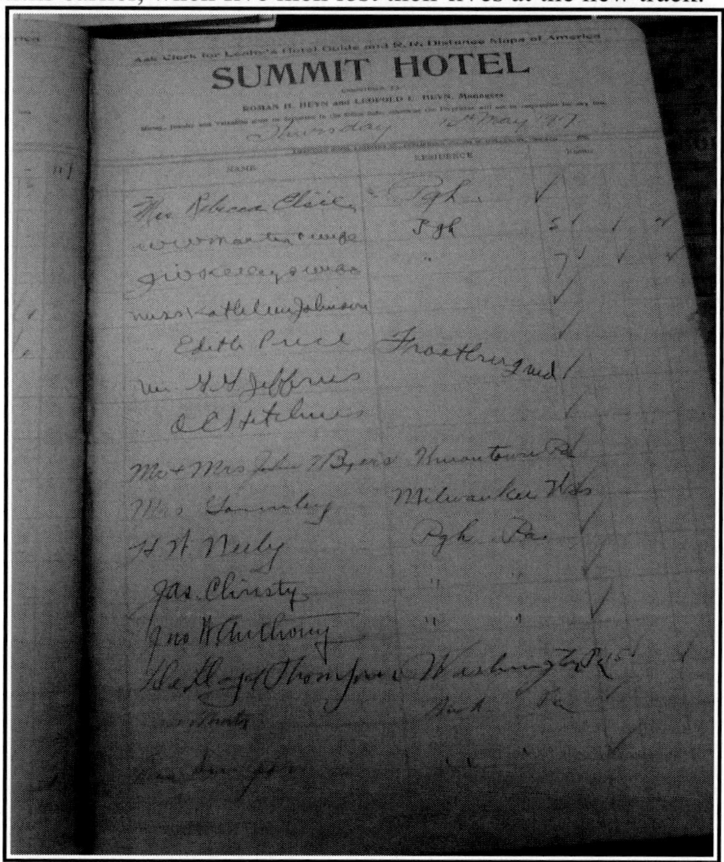

SUMMIT HOTEL

Aviator DeLloyd Thompson of Washington, Pennsylvania wowed crowds at the races with his flying antics.

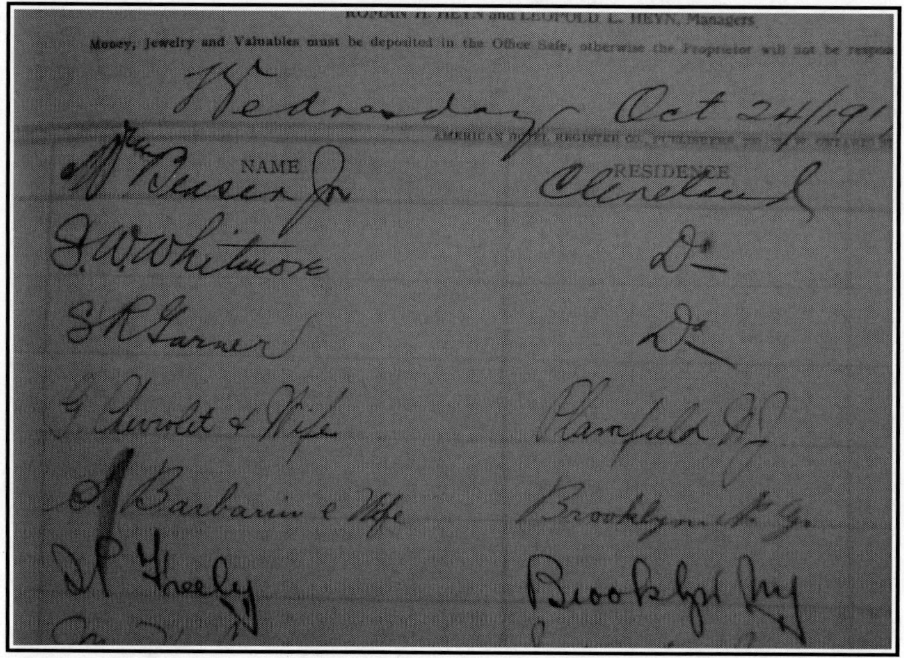
ROMAN H. HEYN and LEOPOLD L. HEYN, Managers

Money, Jewelry and Valuables must be deposited in the Office Safe, otherwise the Proprietor will not be respon

Wednesday Oct 24/191

AMERICAN HOTEL REGISTER CO., PUBLISHERS

NAME	RESIDENCE
Wm Beaser Jr	Cleveland
G. W. Whitmore	Do
S R Garner	Do
G. Chevrolet & Wife	Plainfield NJ
A Barbarin & Wife	Brooklyn NY
D P Freely	Brooklyn NY

Gaston Chevrolet and his wife slept here for the Autumn Classic race of 1917. Gaston hit the fence along the back wall of the track and was thrown out of the #44 Frontenac on lap #135.

"I was a hotel brat," said Karen Harris, who grew up at the Summit Hotel. "As a child, I stood by the front desk waiting for the doors to open to see who I could make friends with." Karen's parents, Eunice and Don Shoemaker, had been managing the Bedford Springs Resort when they first encountered the Summit Inn opportunity. It was 1957. The hotel had its heyday and needed extensive tender loving care. The hotel got lucky when the Shoemakers arrived with their vision and tenacity. The rooms were run down. They had well to do friends in Bedford who wanted to visit, but they were embarrassed to invite them for a stay until they remodeled several of the rooms.

Through the years, their hard earned profits were reinvested into the renovation and upkeep of the historic gem the Shoemakers grew to love. Thirty nine years after their arrival, the Pennsylvania Travel Council named Don the "Distinguished Hotelier of the Year". He passed away the next year, just before his redesigned banquet hall was completed. It was 1997 when the grand porch hotel lost its proprietor. Visitors would no longer encounter Don in the lobby among Stickley-designed furniture where so many famous men gathered.

Karen and Randall Harris had taken over the management of the resort until retiring several years ago. Karen's daughter, Amanda, along with husband, Jeremy are now managing the family business and are having a great time. They just put in a new pool, hot tub and shower house. The Animal Planet's Tree House Masters constructed their popular Black Bear Bungalow Tree House with its vast view. This, in addition to the view from the porch and pool, brings travelers and locals back year after year for weddings, lunch, dinner, meetings, golf, and vacation.

"We are a different type of resort," Karen smiled. With over 1,000 acres of property, the family mulls over future developments. Years ago you could ski here. Today, the Summit Inn is delighted to remain "your home in the mountains."

CHAPTER 2

HOPWOOD/ UNIONTOWN AREA LEGENDS

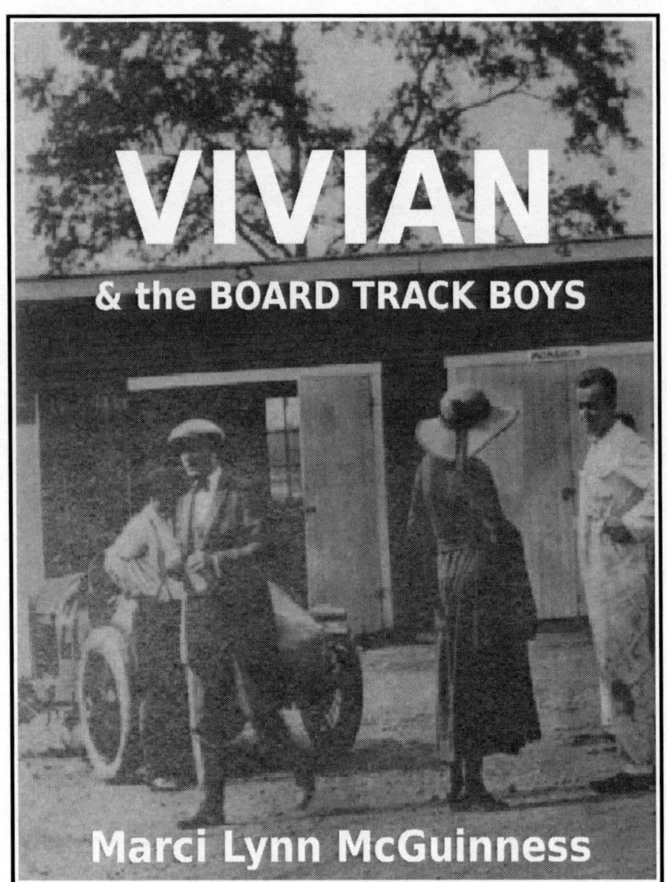

GIRL TO COMPETE IN LONG AUTOMOBILE RACE.

PHILADELPHIA, April 8.—The only permission ever granted to a woman auto driver to compete in the races at Indianapolis has been won by Miss Vivian Prescott of 904 North Broad street, this city, the daring young driver who created a sensation at the Vanderbilt Cup races by taking part in the death-dealing course disguised as a mechanician and riding with Neil Whalen, the National driver.

A century ago, a silent film star made the Uniontown Speedway board track famous. This work of fiction by Marci McGuinness was inspired by her true story.

Although I was a famous actress, I was not allowed to ride in my husband's car. Requesting permission would have given the Vanderbilt Cup Racing Commission the chance to turn me down. Luckily, Neil was adventurous. We devised a plan the day we met George Titlow at the Brunot Island Race Track in Pittsburgh. It was his laugh that drew us to the crowd surrounding Louis Chevrolet and Barney Oldfield. As we approached, the men turned toward us. George spoke first.

"Miss Prescott, I am a true fan of your films," he said. I nodded, smiled.

To Neil, "Great driving today, Mr. Whalen."

"Call me Neil. If I drove better this crowd would be around me." They all laughed and shook hands.

"I am George Titlow, and thrilled to meet you both. We will be going to Uniontown in the Marietta brothers railroad car if you would like to join us."

"Coal country!" I quipped.

"I own the most lavish hotel in Western Pennsylvania, the Titlow," he promised, bowing to me. "Please join us. I am at your service."

Rockwell Marietta said, "He will not take no for an answer, Ma'am. It is the key to his success, and ours."

"We would love to, wouldn't we, Neil?"

"Most assuredly. I know of the Titlow Hotel. We are from Philadelphia where they strive to outdo you."

George laughed for some time. "Then you will join us?"

Neil clapped George on the back. "You do know how to put a party together, George."

Barney Oldfield came out from the middle of the crowd where he was signing autographs. "Barney!" I called to him. We were old friends. His parents were in the entertainment business and now he was promoting the racing industry on Broadway and in a film. He hugged me, not something men did with women in public during the early 1900's. It would have been more appropriate to kiss my cheek, but Barney was anything but appropriate.

"Well, now, Viv, aren't we the rose among so many thorns?"

He took my elbow and walked me to the train as if we had planned the trip together, but he did not board. Once guests were mingling in the dining area of the rail car, George asked Neil and I to his table. I was the only woman among these powerful, lovely men, except for J.V. Thompson's wife, Hunny. We had met them in New York earlier that year.

"I wish I could drive a race car," I said to George during our conversation about Neil's driving career.

"As an actress, you could join Oldfield in one of his films," he humored me.

"I was thinking about the Vanderbilt Cup races or at Indy."

He burst out laughing. "I like you very much," he said when he caught his breath.

"Then please call me Viv."

He nodded the affirmative, smiling.

"What is going on here?" Neil asked from my right.

"It seems we are going to find a way to get your wife in a big race."

He looked at us, "Could we sneak her into my car for the Vanderbilt race as mechanic?"

"Now you are talking, man. Of course, through disguise."

He turned to me, "Being an actress, you could do it, of course, but can you do the job? Dispensing fuel is not for the faint of heart."

"Faint, she is not," Neil assured him.

"As a woman of your stature, you may be forgiven after the fact," George smiled.

And so it went. I did dress as Neil's mechanic, dramatically removing my goggles and cap after crossing the finish line in Ormond Beach, Florida. The crowd gasped and officials took us into their office. They were diplomatic and forgiving as George predicted. Although he could not be there that day, he and Neil encouraged me to write to the Indianapolis Speedway for permission to be the first woman to drive on the brick track. I did and I was, after winning many trophies on the sands of Ormond Beach under Barney's tutelage.

"My Anna is very proud of you," George told me in a telegram. We had met and became friends at the Titlow Hotel during that first visit. Neil and I invited them to Philadelphia for a weekend in the city. They accepted, and we showed them a grand time. It was 1912. Two homes, seven children and several businesses kept them tied to Uniontown. The coke boom was in full force there. Neil and I had car dealerships in both Philadelphia and New York. We lived well, but as he eased out of race car driving, we were yearning for new adventures. It seems that each time we met George, history was made.

"You must be our guests for Old Home Week, Vivian," Anna insisted. "George is in charge of entertainment. It will be grand. He is throwing an elaborate parade, has a bi plane pilot hired to fly above us, and is setting up a short race track."

We stayed in a suite on the second floor of the Titlow Hotel for three days. Watching George in action was quite a treat. I always wanted to film him. He was against that idea, but treated us like royalty, giving us a grand tour of the coal and coke region. It was all so exciting, the mines, the coke ovens, the barges shipping it all to Pittsburgh. It was also a sharp contrast to the elaborate parade he threw, which rivaled big city events. Pittsburgh Brewing's six horse team led their Old Home Week Princess to the balcony of the McClelland House Hotel where she was crowned and presented with a diamond ring! George seemed to know everyone who was top of their line. Politicians, businessmen, adventurers, newsmen, they were all there.

The drag race track drew thousands of spectators, with Charlie Johnson of the nearby Standard Garage wowing crowds. They were yelling, "Speed King," at him. George waved him over to us. As soon as we were introduced, with Charlie kissing the back of my hand, he and Neil walked to his garage with their heads together. George watched the men as they crossed the National Road. "What is it?" I asked him. He smiled, took my arm, and we followed them. It was that day when George began organizing the Fayette Automobile Club and annual Summit Mountain Hill Climbs.

George & Charlie Save Uniontown

"What a view, George," Harvey Firestone smiled, standing on top of Summit Mountain with his 'Firestone Tires' banner hung across the finish line. Twenty five thousand people lined the treacherous 3-mile hill for the 3rd annual Summit Mountain Hill Climb. Men were sitting and standing on telephone poles, signs, and hillsides. The Summit Hotel was filled past capacity inside and out as the first motorcycle in history, a Flying Merkle, topped the knob.

Anna and I were sitting in George's car. The men were standing in the hot sun. As the Charleroi boy and his motorcycle made it successfully over the mountain, the feat was so exciting that Dr. Van Kirk, who was standing next to George, fell dead of a heart attack. Earlier that day, a nineteen year old boy was killed during practice. It seemed AAA changed the red flag to mean "All's Clear" when it always meant "Danger," unbeknownst to the Pittsburgh driver. He died in George's arms.

Then, Uniontown's fastest driver, Charlie Johnson, beat Indy 500 winner, Ralph DePalma. Charlie's ego inflated immediately while George was heartsick over the deaths. He called a press conference to berate the AAA for not alerting all drivers of the flag change.

Charlie spoke against George's remarks and broke away from his long-time mentor, even forming his own auto club. It was awful. Charlie still frequented the Titlow. George still backed Charlie's race cars, but they did not talk.

So, George was planning the biggest hill climb race the area had ever witnessed for spring 1916, bringing in all professional drivers. The Playa del Rey board track in California had burnt. The Brunot Island dirt track in Pittsburgh closed up. George went after his friends in high places, and so did Neil and I, to make this a national event. DePalma meant to beat Charlie this time. He said so in the newspapers. The challenge was set. Uniontown was at a fever pitch of excitement. You could feel it in the air.

Just days before the race, the state

transportation department outlawed the hill climb. We had all just been to the wooden track in Brooklyn. Charlie, with his new auto club behind him, George included, collected money from coal barons, film executives, and auto moguls from all over the country. By now, George's friends were Charlie's friends. The two men still did not speak, but worked alongside each other to organize a money making track.

J.V. Thompson, local banker and coal baron, was going bankrupt, taking dozens of millionaires with him thanks to Henry Frick and J.V.'s ex wife. The town that reined as the richest in the country, wobbled financially. George and Charlie saw a chance to keep the boom going. Neil and I helped them. We were having the time of our lives. Could see what could be. We kept a suite at the hotel full time for years to come.

When I sent "Uncle" Carl Laemmle a telegram about the new board track, he was building Universal Film Studio in Hollywood. He just moved his production company west from New York, but I knew he would want in on this. Henry Ford and Tom Edison were with him when he received my note. It was the three of them who came up with the idea of the annual Universal Film Trophy for the big race. Laemmle said, "I have a silversmith who can craft you a masterpiece the world will not forget, faster than they can build that track."

He was wrong. Charlie Johnson and George Titlow worked furiously, getting the track built in two months time. It took a week longer to craft the trophy. Most of the men who were now racing cars, started by racing bicycles. These early Speed Kings included Charlie and old friend, Jack Prince. Jack was now designing the wooden race tracks. This evolved into the fastest auto racing anywhere. So, we all invested in getting the mile and an eighth board track built and promoted in record time. Those who had planned on attending the canceled hill climb were more than ready to see the country's newest wooden track, sitting in the most beautiful part of Pennsylvania.

We got rained out over Thanksgiving when the Preliminary Opening Race was scheduled. It was December 2nd by the time conditions became plausible. The men were both on edge and full of themselves. Anna and I spent much of that week at their Stone House in the mountains. The countryside became increasingly celebratory as the drivers, crews and cars arrived. Special trains brought thousands of spectators from major cities. Drivers were doing practice runs up the mountain.

Neil had driven at Indy for three years, so it was no trouble getting all the top drivers to the new track. Fred and August Duesenberg, Louis, Arthur and Gaston Chevrolet, Tommy Milton, Ralph DePalma, Hughie Hughes, Frank Galvin, they all came to win the Universal Film Trophy. It was worth $3,000. and the top cash prize was $1,000.

I still give thanks that Anna and I stayed in the box seats off the grand stand during that first Universal Race. Hughie Hughes initially gave a special performance in his 12 cylinder Sunbeam. We twirled our parasols and waved at the cameras, until the Hoskins team of Hughes and Galvin hit each other on the track. Hughes ended up in the infield. We could see George running to him, pulling him out of the car. The crowd cheered as Hughes waved to us all. He was uninjured. They walked quickly to the press stand but Galvin had lost control. We could see him barreling toward them. Poor Anna! She screamed George's name as the car hit Hughes. Charlie dove on George, saving his life as Galvin plowed into the press stand. It collapsed with over a hundred people tumbling and screaming. Louis Chevrolet won the race, unaware of the horror that was going on. We could see Hughes and several of them were dead, and many injured.

A Universal Film cameraman ran in to film it all up-close, but was removed from the property by security. He did return after things calmed down. Universal filmed all the races through the years, playing the movies at the Lyric Theater downtown, including what he shot from that day.

The race went on and in May, the grand opener brought in Barney Oldfield and his Golden Submarine. He was so famous that tracks worldwide paid him $4,000. just to show up. He didn't have to race, but he did. Here he arrived in his own special railroad car, hauling the first race car with a roof. It was built by Miller and Offenhauser in Los Angeles. The Duesenbergs stared at it for hours. Men climbed all over it as they unloaded it.

It was a great Grand Opening day in 1917. No injuries occurred. A young unknown, Billy Taylor, won the big race. Uniontown was on the map as an internationally competitive racing town now. The Titlow Hotel, Summit Inn and 16 more Uniontown hotels were enjoying remarkable profits. Everyone who had a room to rent to visitors, did so. George said they baked 900 loaves of bread that day, and served more rye than on the hotel's grand opening day when 1500 attended and the drinks were free.

It was such fun, but I was thankful for Anna. She was really the only woman friend I had in the area. I was usually with Neil, surrounded by his racing comrades. It was an enviable position, I know, but Anna and I would get away from the fray and hide at the Stone House for spells of time, to recharge. Being a celebrity helped keep the complaints down from other females and the men about my presence. I was privileged to do things women were "not supposed" to do in those days. Our investment of money, time, and contacts helped, too. Neil ran the show as manager of events and flagman. George handled the entertainment, again bringing in bi planes to wow the crowds between races. Charlie charmed investors, spectators, drivers, and sometimes even me.

He worked very hard to get the track open and running. He offered his garage to several competing drivers, just like he did for DePalma the year before. Charlie was dealing Packards now, too. George had financed the business several years ago. I did not know the details, but watching the men bring the town out of a bust situation from J.V.'s bank collapse was quite something. Over forty five thousand people filled the town, many of them wealthy. All businesses were thriving. The downtown streets bustled. Theaters filled, some were showing my films.

George was a family man, although his Vice Presidency of the National Hotel Association took him to every large city in the country, speaking before powerful peers. Charlie had never married, but always had a lassie on his arm, oftentimes, each arm. He had a way with people. A true salesman.

I almost forgot about the long distance races Charlie took on. He was quite famous around the country now for beating DePalma, but that last run from the Uniontown Elks to the Baltimore Elks made him a household name, like Oldfield and Ford. He was a big name now and meant to use it.

J.V.'s bank had just gone down, taking many area businessmen with it. Johnson's customers were not paying him on time if at all. He was getting into financial trouble because of this trickle down, and there was a warrant out for his arrest. He needed a co pilot for the road race, but his Speed King antics had scared off many of his friends. The sheriff agreed to ride with him, and did, with the warrant in his pocket. The Baltimore Elks had a grand welcome for the men, but nothing like Uniontown. There was a circus in town, so when they arrived home after just over 11 hours driving time, they were put up on an elephant and run through the Elks front door. Charlie fell off. This was his last hurrah as a race car driver. George paid his fines behind closed doors, and the men built the nation's fastest race track.

Being a silent film actress, people were used to me just smiling and batting my eyes. This art has allowed me to listen to many a high powered conversation between the major industrialists of our time. Neil loved this benefit. It was like being married to an inside stock trader, he always said. I was very often the only woman among dozens of men, drivers, mechanics, sponsors. The Duesenberg brothers, the Chevrolets, all the teams helped each other get their cars right. Then they raced against each other with all they had. It was a proving ground for early auto racing, and an awful lot of laughs, too, even with World War I on.

Neil was having the time of his life but he did get called to service for a short time. The national newspapers covered every race. He ran the show, and what a show it always was. In 1919, the Duesenberg team of Tommy Milton and Jimmy Murphy set 52 AAA speed records. By then, a lot of the early mechanics were drivers, the best in the world. The rivalries were interesting, too. DePalma and Oldfield didn't care for each other over a Ford sponsorship. Murphy pulled away from Milton, then became the first American to win the French Gran Prix. And George's ethics were rubbed more raw each year as Charlie's ego expanded.

In 1920, 50,000 spectators filled the stands. It was the biggest race in America that year. Afterward, Charlie promised to use the proceeds to repair the track. There were holes big enough for the local boys to put their heads up through from under the boards! An illustrator drew the scene for the newspapers. George was enraged. During a photo shoot for a new Black & Decker compressor, over 100 men gathered around the Duesenberg team cars. I got in the picture. It was a wonderful time, except that I also witnessed an exchange between George and Charlie. After 5 years of silence, they spoke. Well, George spoke.

"We need to act immediately and get this track repaired. The town depends on it," he said leaning very close to Charlie's face. They locked eyes. The Speed King nodded affirmatively.

I wondered if anyone else saw or heard this. I could not look away. They were behind the crowd. The camera's flash went off several times before Charlie walked away, meeting up with a young, beautiful woman.

I had never had a brother, so being a part of, and watching, the interaction of the Chevrolet and Duesenberg brothers, was such fun to me. Louis loved Gaston, Henry and Arthur dearly. It was obvious. He was designing Gaston a new race car as a surprise. In the pits all the race teams worked hard, laughing, building parts as needed, sharing insights, making history. Uncle Carl brought several rail cars filled with actresses, crew, friends, and family from L.A. to every race. There were fabulous parties before, during and after the races.

George was right to be after Charlie, as it turned out. I never understood why the Uniontown Speedway Association entrusted most of the financial responsibility to the charming cad, but they did. Senator Crow was their lawyer. They had a treasurer and all, but I often witnessed "investors" walking into the box office, pocketing a handful of cash from one of the full wooden barrels, and going about their day. They were wildcat times, and we all paid the price for playing more than working at our beloved track.

The day before the 1922 race, KDKA radio interviewed Barney, Jimmy Murphy and many of the drivers for the first time. The Uniontown Speedway Association also filed for bankruptcy. The owners of the property pulled the lease out from under us, but Charlie quickly stopped their action. The race went on. Had I paid better attention, maybe I could have stopped him. Charlie was dressed casually, with sun glasses, and no suit jacket or hat that last race. We all knew he was under stress, but no one was aware of his plan. The signs were there, though. He lost weight and was on edge. After the race, he disappeared.

It was Uncle Carl who used his connections in Cuba to locate Charlie. He had taken the money from the last race, and went into hiding. Weeks later, Senator Crow died. His procession passed by the deserted track. We watched as a poor family pulled boards from "Death's Curve", on our way to the cemetery. George sold his beloved Titlow Hotel in the midst of Uniontown's depression and prohibition saying, "You can not run a hotel without spirits." Rockwell passed on that same year.

George and Anna visited us in the city occasionally, but we never returned to Uniontown. Other tracks opened and closed. We stayed out of the business end of them, just watching and enjoying the thrill. George, always the adventurer, flew over the Himalayas with Lowell Thomas.

Louis Chevrolet died penniless. Fred Duesenberg passed away a few weeks after his crash while doing a speed test on Route 30 near the Jennerstown, Pennsylvania racetrack, in 1932.

Charlie returned to Uniontown in 1940 with a wife named Edna. His family called her "crass." At the opening race of the New Bryson's Uniontown Speedway, which was built in the infield of the old board track, Charlie spoke, dedicating the facility. George was in the crowd with his daughter. Using his cane, he moved as quickly as he could toward the officials booth. George had been living in a nearby town for several years. This was the first he knew of Charlie's return. The men had words when they met outside the booth. Two days later, George had a massive heart attack in his lawyer's office. He was livid about Charlie's return to Uniontown. Charlie started a small brewery, paid his workers in worthless scrip, took off to Oklahoma, and struck oil. Neil died that year, too, but I have my memories.

NOTE: Vivian Prescott made 202 silent films. She was instrumental in bringing Universal Films to the Uniontown Speedway board track, 1916 – 1922.

A Uniontown Speedway Board Track Collection...

As I continue my local historical research, people often come to me with very interesting photographs. They normally do not know who the people are, and that is where I come in. After over three decades of meeting local characters of bygone eras in old photos, I can oftentimes match one picture up with another and identify (to the best of my ability) photographs that would otherwise be long forgotten and destroyed. This is the scenario that leads to finds like this one. While speaking with Karen Harris and her daughters, Amanda and Kristie, at the Summit Inn, they asked if I would take a look at a dozen or so photos that had been torn in half. They were 8 x 10's. I laughed when I saw Barney Oldfield big as life in a car I can not pinpoint (next page).

Here they are...

Below, Top: Jimmy Miller, Duesenberg driver, at the Uniontown Speedway board track, June 17, 1922, final race. He came in third this day.

Below, Bottom: Eddie O'Donnel's Duesenberg, June 21, 1920.

Below, L-R: June 21, 1920, Jimmy Murphy and his #9 Duesenberg, Neil Whalen (Flagman), Gaston Chevrolet in his new #1 Frontenac. His older brother, Louis, built this car for him as a gift just a few months earlier. A few months later, Gaston was killed in the car in Beverly Hills. Louis, broken-hearted, continued running his team, but never drove again.

Tommy Milton (left) in his Duesenberg at the Uniontown Speedway board track, 1917.

This is Barney Oldfield in his Delage, 1917, at the Uniontown Speedway board track. I kept the photograph in the condition it was found to show that someone tore it in half for disposal. Bob McGarvey of McGarvey's Photo in Uniontown, PA is repairing the collection to be displayed at the Summit Hotel.

Below: Notice the U.F.C. Universal Film Company copyright at bottom and big © to the right. The Olson Driver here is mechanic, William Claus with Bert Watson (Driver in race), Preliminary Opening Race, December, 2, 1916.

Bryson's Uniontown Speedway, Est. 1940

Is this the opening race at the Bryson track? I do not know. Cars #2 and #4 prepare for the contest to the right. In the opener, Eddie Zaluckle of Detroit drove a Dreyer Special here. The announcer is on the stand. Is Charlie Johnson there? At the opening race, after 18 years of hiding in Cuba because he robbed the board track investors (1922), Johnson spoke at the dedication ceremony. Two days later, Titlow, Johnson's former mentor, died in his lawyers office. More about that in the *Vivian & the Board Track Boys* story in this book.

My dear friend, Bill Scott, called one day. "I found some photographs of the 1940's Bryson track," he said. "I can't identify any of them. They are very small shots taken from far away. It might not be much." We met at Herring's Diner in Hopwood where we took a very close look at them. The year before, Bill had given me a piece of memorabilia from the old Lucky Teter shows that were held at the track. Lucky jumped buses with motorcycles and brought in big crowds.

After studying one of the photographs he had in a clear folder, I said, "That is your buddy, Lucky. It says so on the buses and trailers here." So, we are happy to show you these photos as it has been difficult to find many from the Bryson days other than the few I have in my earlier book, *Yesteryear at the Uniontown Speedway.* Several of these shots show the track under construction. The half mile dirt track was built in the infield of the old 1 1/8 mile wooden track. It had asphalt turns. The public was thrilled to welcome racing back to town.

Earl "Lucky" Teter and his Hell Riders are all lined up for a show at Bryson's Uniontown Speedway. Lucky and his stunt team ran a traveling attraction that jumped buses and trailer trucks with cars and motorcycles. "Lucky" lost his life in one such feat in 1942. It was supposed to be his last jump before joining the Army and enlisting in World War II.

More Bryson's Uniontown Speedway...

Coal Barons, Pirates, Patch Teams, Play Ball!

John Burns of Buffington signs on with the Pirates farm team, late 1940's.

Patch Produces Coal Baron Ball Team Center-fielder

Note: After the Bryson track of the early 1940's, the Uniontown Speedway infield was home to the Coal Baron Ball team.

They have been married an impressive 61 years. John Burns was born in the coal patch called "Palmer", an old Frick company town on the Monongahela River (Adah, PA), but grew up nearby in their Buffington home in the middle of a family of 16 children, eight boys and eight girls. One day he spotted Rose in her yard in nearby Lambert. He stopped the car. They married 6 months later. Today, John is the eldest of his living siblings at 86 years old. (Written in 2013).

I asked what they ate as children. "Coffee soup and bread," he laughed. "We spent most of our time playing ball."

John and his brothers, Glenn and Regis, all played for Pirate farm teams in the late 1940's. Bill Scott of Hopwood told me about John because we have been trying to identify the 1948 Coal Baron ball team photograph that has been in my *Yesteryear at the Uniontown Speedway* book since 1996. John played for the Coal Barons in 1949, so these men still remain a mystery.

At 19 years old, John signed on with the Greenville, Alabama Pirate Farm Team. "We were paid $150. per month. We ate minced ham and grabbed watermelons along the road. It's not enough to live on." His bothers played on Pirate teams in Texas and New Mexico.

"The three of us still living all played baseball," John reminisced. "Regis was the home-run guy. He would run past the fence and people handed him tips through the gaps as he ran into home plate."

"One time when he played against us," Glenn laughed. "I set it up so Regis could get an inside the park home run and get the tip money."

"It started when Major League scouts came to Uniontown at Baile Park. Niagara Falls was playing the Coal Barons. The manager signed Glenn right away. I had signed with the Pirates already."

Glenn was 17 years old to John's 19. Regis was younger than them, at 15 yrs old when he went to the southwest to play ball. Chicken John, named for his love of fried chicken, had a 365 batting average, so they moved him to Uniontown's Coal Baron ball team in 1949. He played there for three months before being sent to York.

"In 1950, I played against Willie Mays. He was on the Giants Farm Team in Trenton, NJ. I broke my hand that year and was sent home."

Robena Mine was happy to see him return. "We will give you a job in the mines if you play on our baseball team," he was told. "We had a good team. I played for them three years." It was on his way home from one of these games that he spotted Rose in her white shorts.

They married in 1952. "After Robena, I played for Buffington, Keister, then Continental."

"The coal ash at the Keister field got the kids so dirty. It would be all over their faces, head to toe," Rose quipped. "I collected the money at the gate in Robena and took in thousands," she said shaking her head up and down.

In 1966, John was buried to the waist, face down, in a mine roof fall. "Jim Nagy of Connellsville pulled me out. He saved my life. Frank McKuka, our boss, did not make out as well. We lost him that day." They showed me the articles about John and his brush with death, along with ball team clips.

Today, John has a do nut for breakfast each morning. "He is a great husband," Rose said. "He sets and colors my hair, puts it up in curlers. He does the dishes, washes the clothes. He helps me."

"I roomed with Trader Jack McKeon in spring training. He became a World Series winning, major league manager. We still go to Pirate games together.

When I played, the manager made more money than the players. I was born 50 years too soon or you would be talking to a millionaire a few times over. I was a line drive hitter and I could steal bases. Glen was a long ball hitter. I liked it. Good and plenty, you know?"

Note: McGuinness wrote this column in 2013 after an interview with John, Rose and Glenn Burns.

Hall of Famer, Bill Scott

Bill Scott, All Star, LeMont Ball Team, 1955.

Bill Scott (right) Pal's Club Fay West Ball League, 1959/60.

For 20 years, Bill Scott of Hopwood, has contributed to my history projects. It started with the first Uniontown Speedway board track book and continues today. He was running the sweeper when I arrived to interview him for this column. Artifacts, albums, and news articles were organized in the living room. Since we had been talking baseball a lot lately, I asked, "When did you play your first baseball game"?

"I got interested in 1946 listening to the Boston Red Sox and St. Louis Cardinals in the World Series.

There were no TV's. My grandmother had a radio. It didn't have a cover on it. When you turned it on you could see the tubes light up. That's where I listened to the game. I ran home from school to hear St. Louis beat the Red Sox and wanted to buy a baseball glove.

My grandfather had a field in back of our house. We made a diamond to play ball using the head board of a bed as a backstop. We only had one ball, so when we lost it, we couldn't play until we found it. All the local kids played. We picked up a game anywhere we could. We used whatever there was to use for a base", he smiled, showing me a Forbes Field home plate from his collection.

A Uniontown *Evening Standard* photograph dated September 9, 1946 headline says, "Hopwood Juniors, They Had a Good Year". The caption goes, "The Hopwood Juniors above won 14 and lost three this season. In front: bat boy (not named), kneeling, Lawrence Gorley, Jerry Hall, Jack Metz, Carl Panko and Joe Guyton (became the first bat boy for the Coal Barons); standing, Johnny Blough, Bill Scott, Joe Kissinger, Bill Doyle, and Chuck Mahoney. Manager John Show".

"When I was 14 our Junior County League team was called the Hopwood Exchange".

Six years later a scout spotted Scott. He recommended him to Cy Morgan, who signed him to train in the Tipton, Georgia farm league in the class D Florida-Georgia circuit.

"They cut me in spring training after 3-4 weeks but that's where I learned everything. The guys who taught me down there played in the major leagues. Taught me how to play the infield. Paul Owens, who ended up being the manager of the Phillies, taught me how to play the outfield. You learned something new everyday".

In a 1959 *Evening Standard* column called "Sports Standard" by Tod Trent, he interviewed Coolspring County League Champions Manager, Carmen Galderisi. "Buck Grover was the ace of the staff with 14 – 0 record, 193 strike-outs in 121 2/3 innings of pitching. Then there was Bill Scott who during the season played all nine positions at one time or another to stamp himself as one of the most versatile sandlot performers around these parts. Scott's offensive contributions included a team leading total of 70 hits and his 41 runs batted in tied him with Andy Machusko for the team leadership in that department. During the playoffs, he slammed the ball at a .400 pace".

"Today I read about pitching, footwork, and all that. I wished I had known it back then. I would have been a better pitcher. I was inconsistent. I learned to throw an off-speed pitch my last year playing. I was 45".

Scott's batting average in 1975 for the Dearth team was .408. He has the bat from this year with his teammates signatures, along with his glove and home run baseball. "I hit my last home run with this bat". He also has a bat from the the old neighborhood school. In 1992, he was inducted into the Big Ten Fayette County Sandlot Baseball Hall of Fame.

In 1982 he ran the Pittsburgh Marathon. Three years later he ran the Washington, D.C. Marathon. It is no surprise that he finished both. "I wanted to make it to the Boston Marathon."

As we said our good byes, Bill handed me a very small envelope. In it was a "Lucky Teeter Hell Drivers Lucky Piece". Teeter was a pre Evil Knievel car stunt man who held events at the old Speedway. It never ends.

The Bat Boys of Brownfield

When I interviewed Coal Baron ball player, John Burns, of Buffington, I asked him if he knew who the Bat Boy was in the above 1948 photograph. Since then, I located one a Bat Boy. Tom Roche and his friends of Brownfield, Pennsylvania played at the Coal Baron Baseball team club house in the late 1940's. "The club house was on top of the grand stands of the old wooden speedway", he reminisced. "We were around twelve or thirteen and one of the guys, Sparky Robatin (Front row, far left in above photo), got to be the Coal Baron Bat Boy. They dressed him in a little gray uniform with the number ½ on the back. He was not very big, maybe three foot tall. He lived in House #13 in the patch.

"We used to run across the field. It was about ¾ of a mile from Brownfield. Every night they had a game we would try to get back home before the ball field lights went out. It was really dark without them", he laughed. "We made it a couple times and it was a ways. We ran halfway around the old track, then past a target shooting club, up a path and across both railroad tracks.

"We hung out there all the time. It was a treat to be in the dugout with the players. Bill Hudacsek was my favorite. He was a right fielder that batted to the left side. He lived in Uniontown on Fayette Street across from the Red Head service station. The players would give us broken bats. We nailed them back together. That's how we got all of our baseballs those years, too. When they shagged balls during batting practice, there would be ten or fifteen boys there. They never threw anyone out. They left us stay there once we were in the ballpark. I didn't pay one time to get in on game days."

When I asked why they were allowed in the club house and dug out, he said, " It started with us going over under the bleachers looking for pennies and nickels. Then we sold hot dogs and Tru Aid for Harry Isabel's concession there. Sparky was the home team Bat Boy and Mascot, but the visiting teams never brought one, so about ½ dozen of us got to be Bat Boy numerous times each".

"The first year, 1947, they held an essay-writing contest, 'Why I want to be the Coal Baron Bat Boy'. Joe Griton won and did it that whole season. The last two years Sparky did it".

"It was free to get into the games after the seventh inning", Bill Scott added. "After the Coal Mining team of Isabella beat the Coal Barons, they could not raise the money to play the 1950 season. Addison bought the uniforms they had already ordered. They just blocked out the Uniontown name and wore them. That Isabella was a tough team. The good players would get the day off from the mines if there was a game".

Players on the 1948 Coal Baron ball team included: Hudacsek, Albert William Rolke, Robert Williams, William Alfred Mongiello (Manager), John Joseph Higgins, William McKee, Daniel Patrick Costello, Donald George Runcie, Ezio Bonetti, Calvin Hogue, Anthony Arthur Seqzda, George Joseph Hallow, Robert James Lilko, Marion Lamar Dorton, Lewis John Fisher (Farmington), and Jack Edward umgarner. Bumgarner is the brother of Actor, James Garner.

At the end of this interview, Hopwood's Bill Scott, who is in the Fayette County Sports Hall of Fame himself for playing ball, handed me a small photograph from a 1909 newspaper. It seems there was a Coal Baron Ball Team in Uniontown back then. They were the champions of the Pennsylvania-West Virginia League. The players are: McAleese, Phillips, Rudolph, Cariss, Roberts, Cowan, Carnes, Fletcher, Hilley, Wilson, McCloskey, Gribben, Miller, Wallace and Gibson as Mascot.

When I asked if he played ball, Tom said, "Yes, in the midgets, Pete Yezback, one of the Coal Baron Ball Team owners, I played for him. We played down Bailey Park".

Roche smiled thinking about his youth, "We were around some heroes those years, us kids, and we never wanted for a bat or ball".

Today's Collectors Honor Hill Climbers

Above Left: Charlie Johnson in his 1914 Greyhound Packard. He beat Indy 500 champ, Ralph DePalma in this car on Summit Mountain in 1915. Above Right: Joe Boyer test drives for the 1914 Hill Climb.

For three years (2013 - 2015), the Summit Inn Resort has hosted the commemorative celebration of the early hill climb days. Above left: Dave and Gregg Dahl top the Summit in their Model T. Right: Three antique autos in a row! Bottom: The car show held by the Summit Mountain Early Iron Car Club. It rained this year, but no one cared! A big thanks to all participants.

Reckless Dan Rex

R.C. Bigler aka Reckless Dan Rex was a true Laurel Highland Legend. An amateur in motor vehicle racing, Bigler made a name for himself in the local newspapers when he appeared at racing events in his 1913 Mercer Raceabout. The Uniontown Morning Herald reporting, "Bigler Makes Best Time in Amateur Events" at the 1914 Summit Hill Mountain Hill Climb where R.C. Bigler took first place in two of the events that day. He set the bar for the fastest time up the hill and was awarded the prized Loving Cup (see photo). Bigler's accomplishments in this hill climb were even reported on by the New York Evening Post.

A few months later Bigler again pleased the crowds at the Waynesburg Fairgrounds where in October the Pittsburgh Press reported that "the most thrilling race of the day was the Australian Pursuit" which was won by Bigler. The next day he traveled from Waynesburg PA to Clarksburg WV where he won the Jackson 10 Mile sweepstake.

R.C. Bigler was not only a legend in amateur racing. He also made his mark on the local infrastructure of the time through his construction projects. In order to afford the purchase of his Mercer, Bigler earned his money building bridges, tunnels, and other various public works projects. He built large abutments in Connellsville for the Pennsylvania Railroad, a water reservoir for the Irwin Waterworks, and bridges built in Trafford, Herminie, and Loyalhanna, just to name a few. Unfortunately, the onset of the Great Depression not only dried up the funding capable to pay for these local infrastructure projects it also brought an end to his amateur racing. Roy Charles Bigler had a total of nine children. Many of the descendants of R.C. Bigler live locally and are proud to claim him as our Laurel Highland Legend.

Submitted by Andrew Capets, great-grandson.

More Bad News!

Ed and Lisa Cupp of Hopwood singing with their "More Bad News" band, a mainstay in the mountains and Uniontown, PA area. Taken circa 2013 at a Storey Square Concert.

Years ago at the Highland House (Titlow Tavern and Grille), More Bad News and Lisa's band, the "Crossroads", played separately. The couple married and have been drawing in crowds at area hot spots for decades. About forty years ago in a conversation at the Highland House, Ed said to me (when I talked about going to college for writing), "Just write. They can't teach you that." So I did.

The energy this band exuded is powerful, legendary. I will be sitting them down for an interview for the next volume in this book series.

Phil's Hopwood Tavern

In 1957 there were five taverns in Hopwood,Pennsylvania, the Village Barn, Hopwood Tavern, Felix Tavern, the Speedway, and Corky's. Phil Savini, Sr., was 29 years old when he and his new bride bought the Hopwood Tavern that April. Fifty five years later, he is the oldest business owner in the village, running the only tavern.

"I was 29 going on 40, was brought up disciplined," the 84 year old smiled.

At 11 years old Phil worked as a shoemaker in his older brother's store in Republic, Toni's Shoe Shop. When Toni was drafted to serve in the War in 1943, Phil took over the business. He was 15 years old. Four years later the brothers expanded into a building bought by their father, who owned Savini's Groceries. There they ran a clothing and shoe store called Savini Brothers, until 1953 when Toni sold his share to Phil.

By 1958, Phil was ready to sell the tavern. Running both businesses was exhausting. The tavern stayed open from 7a.m. To 2a.m. for the coal miners and steel workers coming in after their shifts. He told his father, "I am tired. We are newlyweds. It is not fair to my wife. I work all the time, and am in debt."

His father advised, "Everything in life is not fair. Stick it out. Get yourself a pencil and paper. On one side list all you owe. On the other side list the price of the bar. Add 'em up. See what number's highest. My debts were higher than the bar price.

"Dad was a miner before WWII then ran his Mom & Pop store until age 72. He was uneducated but had more common sense than most. He lived to 101 years old."

It seems Phil has adapted his father's practical advise into a very satisfying lifestyle. He sold Savini Brothers in 1958. "I never drew a paycheck from an employer. I have been self-employed all my life, except for my time in the service. I have always had a lot of family support."

Now married 56 years, with four grandchildren, he is happy he listened to his father. "It wasn't easy, but I don't regret it. I am glad to be here."

When I asked if the tavern has changed much these 55 years, he laughed. Everything has been remodeled. The only original thing is the bar rail. Phil also owns the apartment building with the barber shop next door. "I am not sure when this building was constructed, but that one has been standing since 1839." He said that there used to be an A & Pstore and a gas station there in earlier days. You can still make a call for 25 cents from the old phone booth that sits unobtrusively at the end of the bar.

In an age when taverns are closing their doors with alarming speed, it is nice to see a man comfortable in the business. When asked if he enjoys being a tavern owner, he laughed. "I enjoy it now. My customers are good, loyal people. I enjoy them. I hope they enjoy me. It is a nice social life here without the foolishness. When most are young in this business they tolerate more foolishness because they hate to lose a customer. I did not put up with a lot of stuff. We are nice about it, taking people to the side and telling them they will just have to go somewhere else."

Phil remembers the Coal Baron Ball Team that played in the Uniontown Speedway infield nearby. "Isabel Coal Company Team beat them," he smiled. The Coal Barons were tied up with the Pirates then."

Most of the Savini family lives in now Salem Heights. Each morning, Phil meets his 90 year old brother for coffee before opening the tavern. "I value every day I wake up. I'm here today. God willing I will be here tomorrow." (Column written December 2012)

Titlow Tavern & Grille, Est. 1906

George Flavius Tilow was a family man in addition to being Uniontown's most famous entrepreneur. He married Anne Beeson in 1888 and had seven children. Titlow built the posh Titlow Hotel in 1906, catering to the rich and famous. He brought the first car to Uniontown in 1902 and started the Summit Mountain Hill Climbs, riding a wave of national fame until 1922 when his mentor, Charlie Johnson, ran to Cuba with the proceeds from the Uniontown Speedway board track.

Today, Jeff D'Maio runs the historic establishment at 92 West Main Street, always upgrading with an eye to preservation. Forty five years ago, his late father, Charlie, bought the run down hotel Since, they redid three of the four floors back to their former glory, and are modernizing upstairs rooms presently.

The Titlow went through the days of the Highland House when talented bands and radio station WDVE showed Uniontown what rock and roll was. The Titlow Tavern & Grille has become famous as the place to dine in Uniontown. They can also say Bat Man ate there (Michael Keaton) amongst many others. While going through their guest books from the hill climb and Uniontown Speedway days, I found these signatures...

Ford Ed. H.

Notice the signatures at the bottom. This is 1912, before the Uniontown Old Home Week celebration. George Titlow was in charge of entertainment, including a drag strip and enormous parade with many cars. The last two signatures were written by one person. Is this Henry Ford?: Ford, Ed. H. He had no middle name, but his son was Edsel. This may be him disguising his name a bit, written by F. W. Floyd, his traveling partner.

HOTEL TITLOW

D. D. RUSH, Proprietor

WEDNESDAY JUNE 7-16.

New York

C. O. Howley

Scranton Pa

City

W. G. Packard slept here for what was supposed to be the 4th annual Uniontown (Summit Mountain) Hill Climb in 1916. The event was outlawed and the Uniontown Speedway board track was built, running the first race on December 2, 1916.

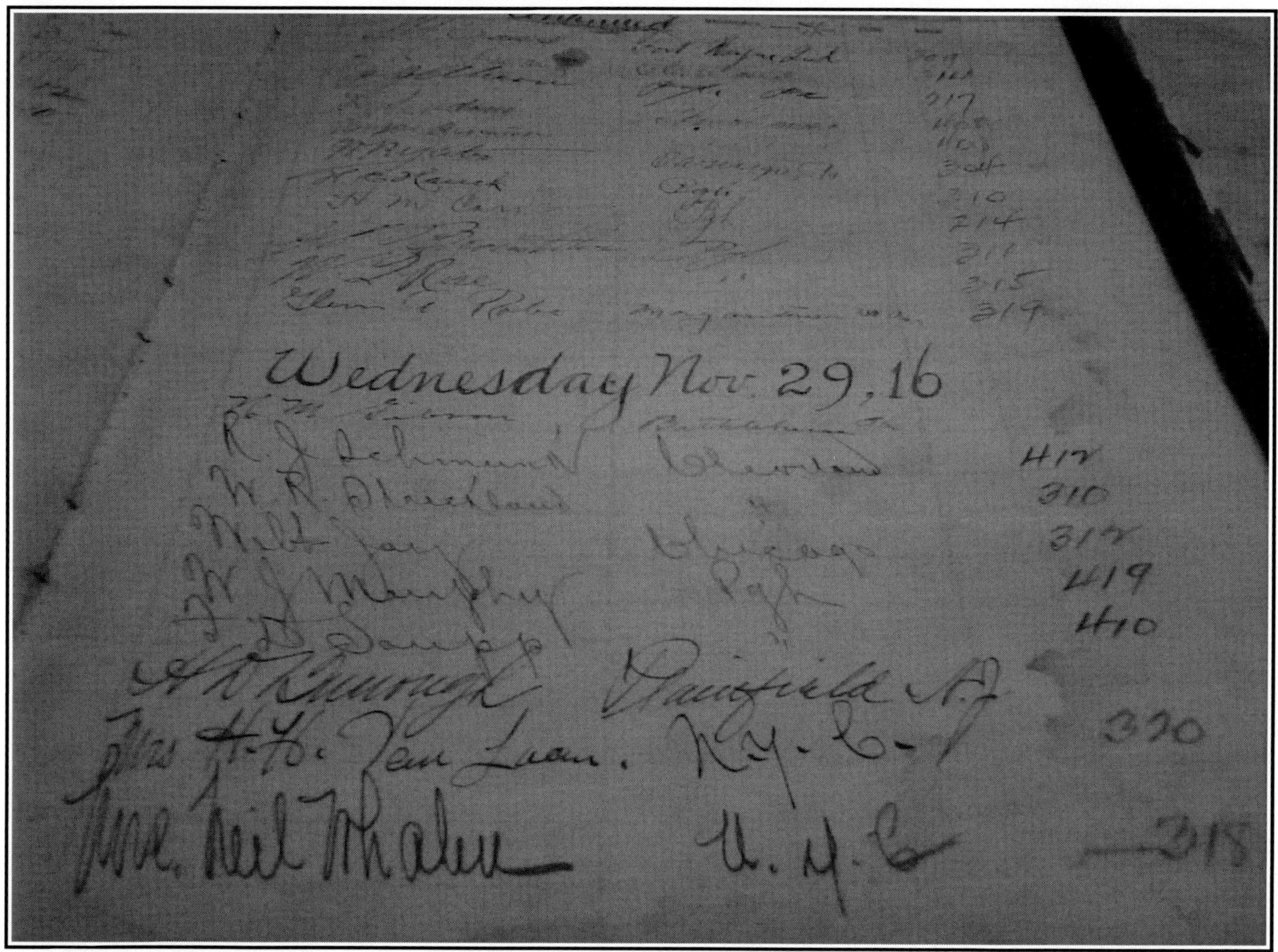

The bottom signature, just days before the Preliminary Opening Race of the Uniontown Speedway board track, is Mrs. Neil Whalen, aka, silent film star, Vivian Prescott. Her husband, Neil, was a driver turned track promoter. He was flagman and manager of events here throughout its 1916 – 1922 rein. They owned car lots in Philadelphia and New York City and brought Universal Films here, who filmed every race and played them at the Lyric Theater in Uniontown. All the names above hers on Nov. 29, 1916 were involved in the races, from Uniontown Speedway Association board members, Public Relations Executives, to Louis Chevrolet's mechanic, H. D. Burough, Plainfield, NJ. Vivian and Neil promoted the track bringing Universal Films here.

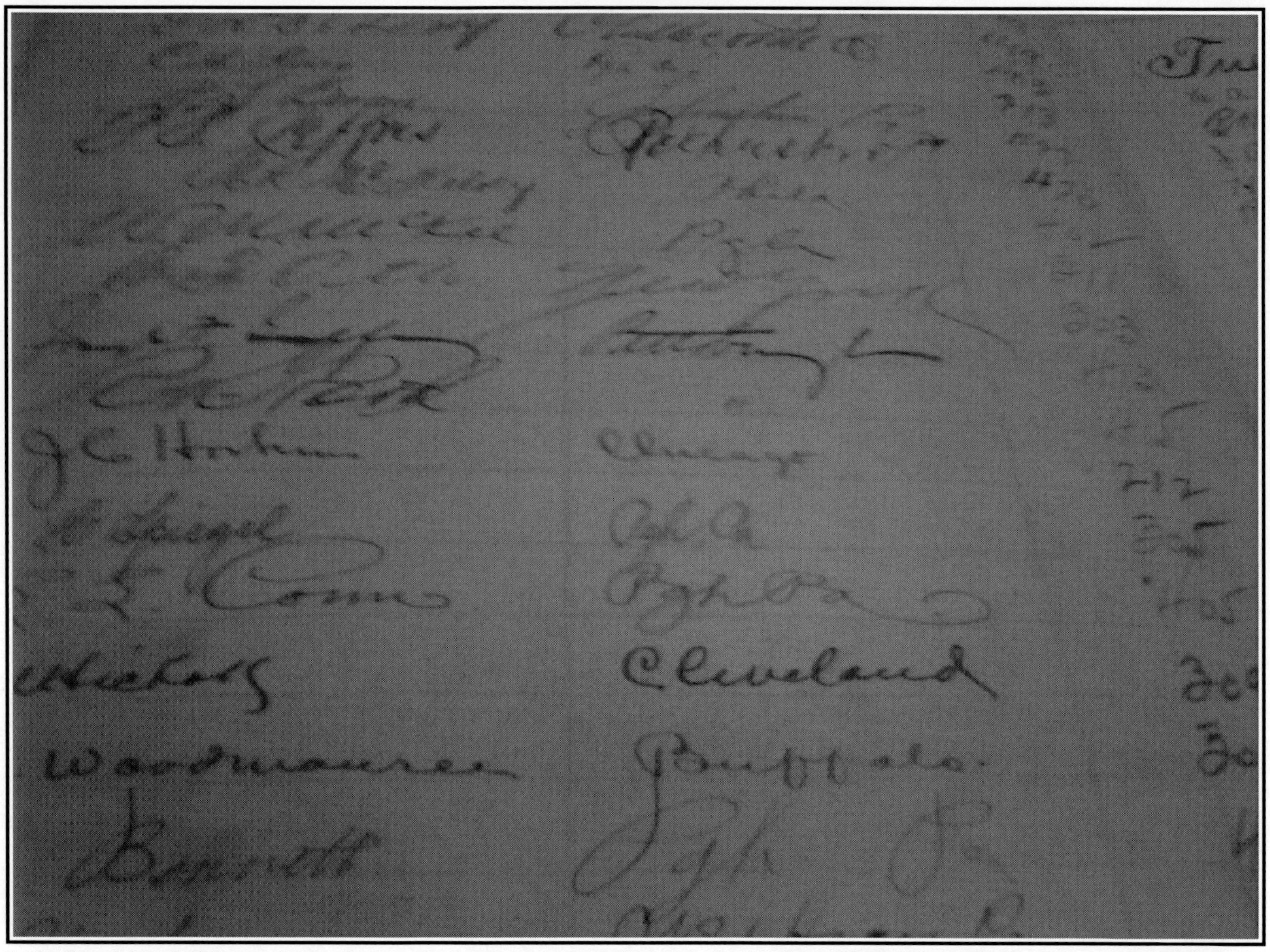

J. C. Hoskins, Chicago based race car team owner slept at the Titlow Hotel for the preliminary race in 1916. He lost two drivers and a mechanic that day in a tragic wreck that killed five and injured 17.

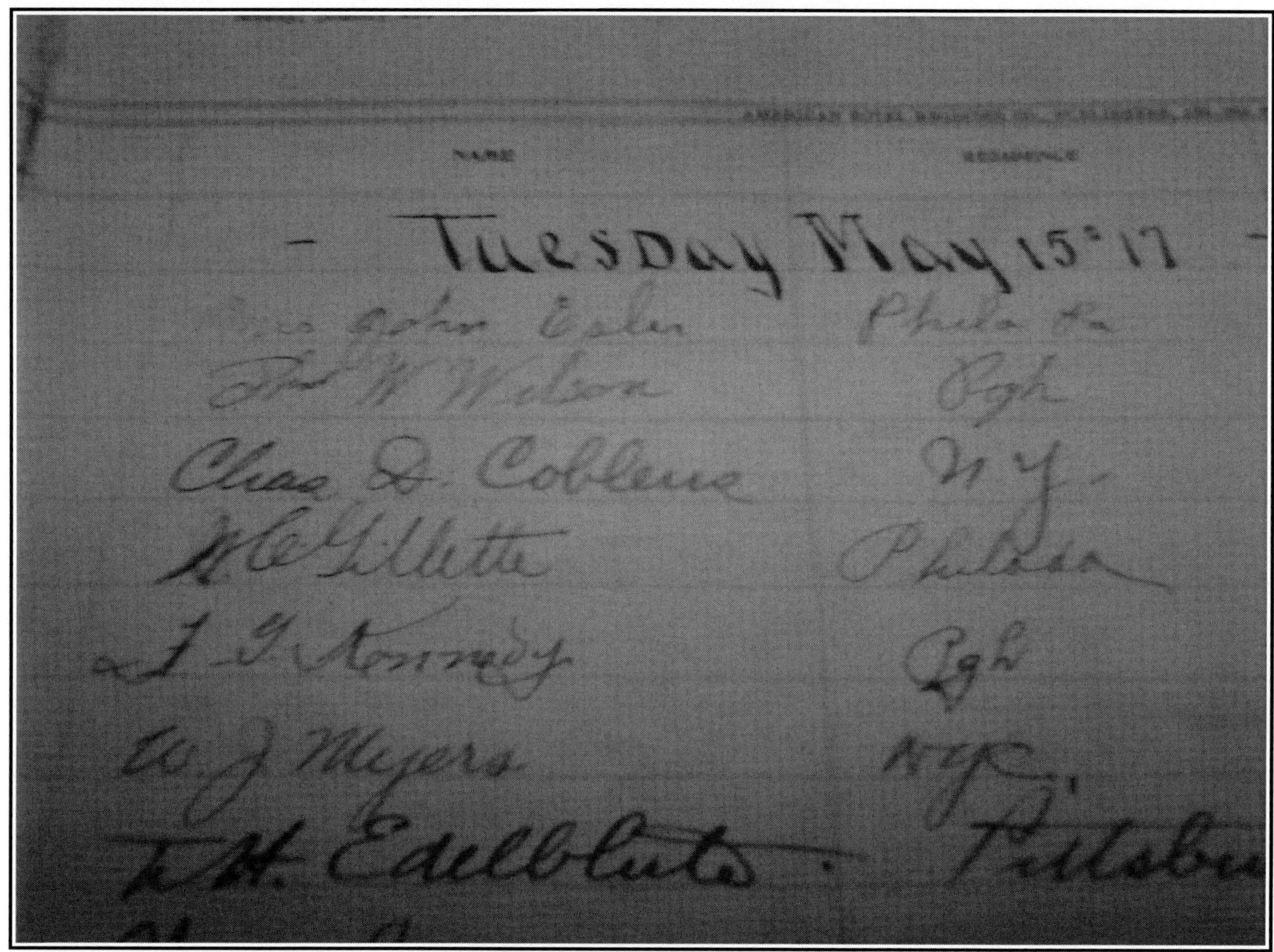

Tuesday May 15° 17

Chas D. Coblens — N.Y.

W C Gillette — Philada

W. J. Meyers — N.Y.

Notice the Gillette signature from Philadelphia. The middle initial is a C. Is this King C. Gillette, inventor of the first safety razor? Pirates infielder, Honus Wagner, was in the original print ad in 1910 for the new razor when it hit the market and changed people's lives. This is five days after the Grand Opening board track race at the Uniontown Speedway.

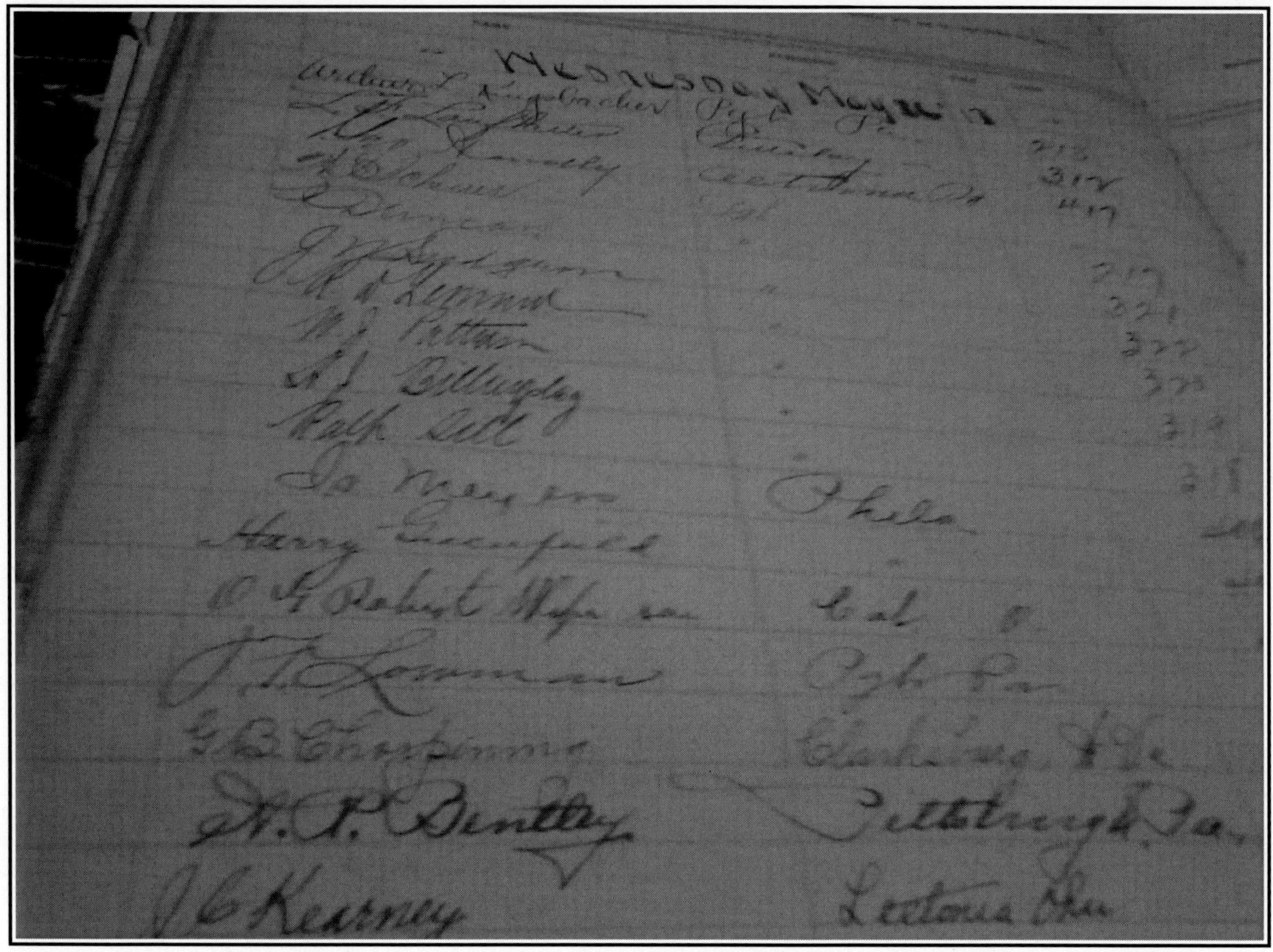

H. P. Bentley arrived at the Titlow Hotel the day after Gillette, in the wake of the Grand Opening Universal Film Race, along with a whole slew of Pittsburghers. The Titlow rocked on.

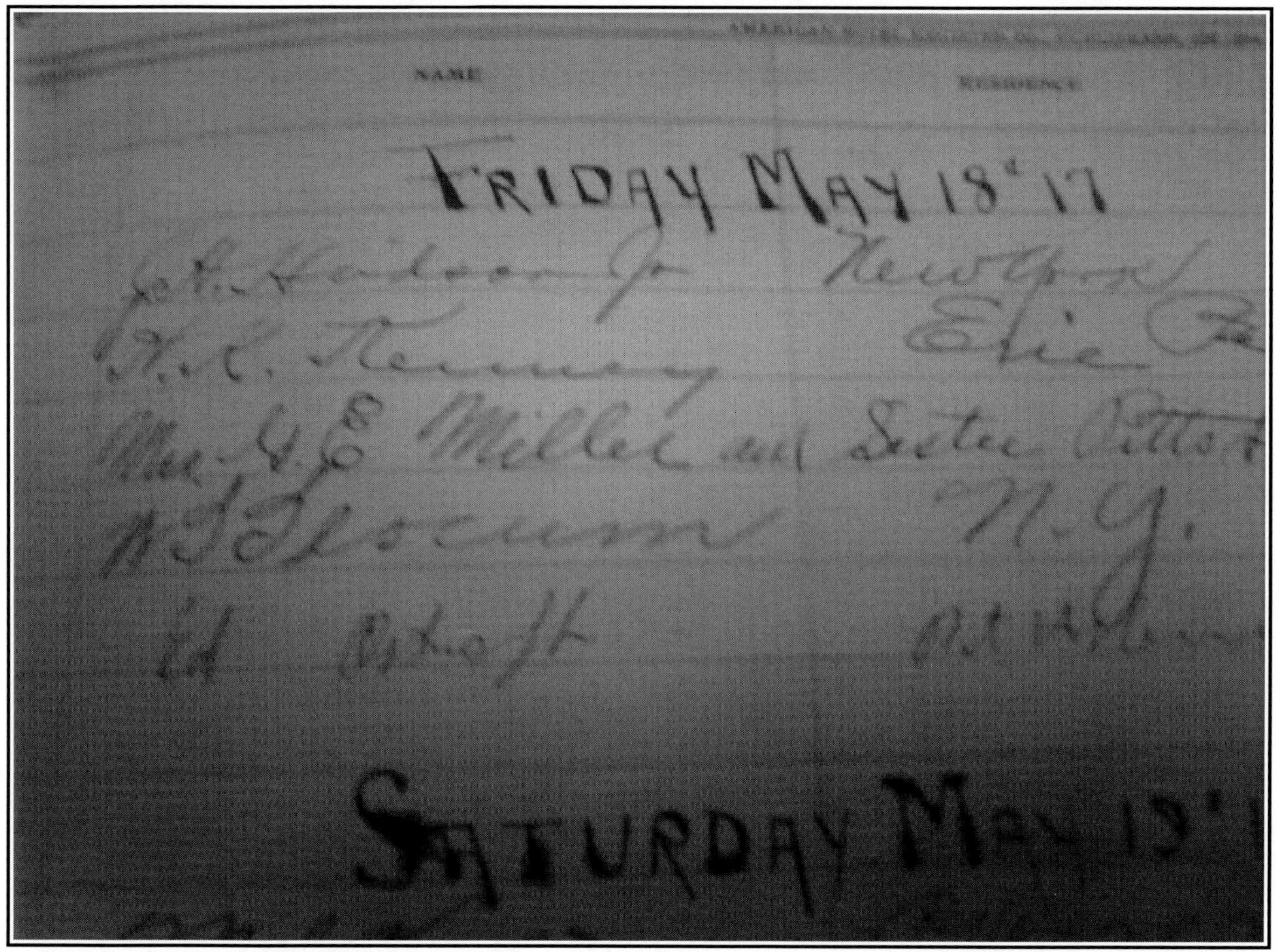

NAME	RESIDENCE

FRIDAY MAY 18th 17

Erie

N. Y.

SATURDAY MAY 19

J. H. Hudson arrived the day after Bentley. Titlow must have been holding court on the fourth floor, where big business was conducted throughout the coal and coke boom and 10 year race rein.

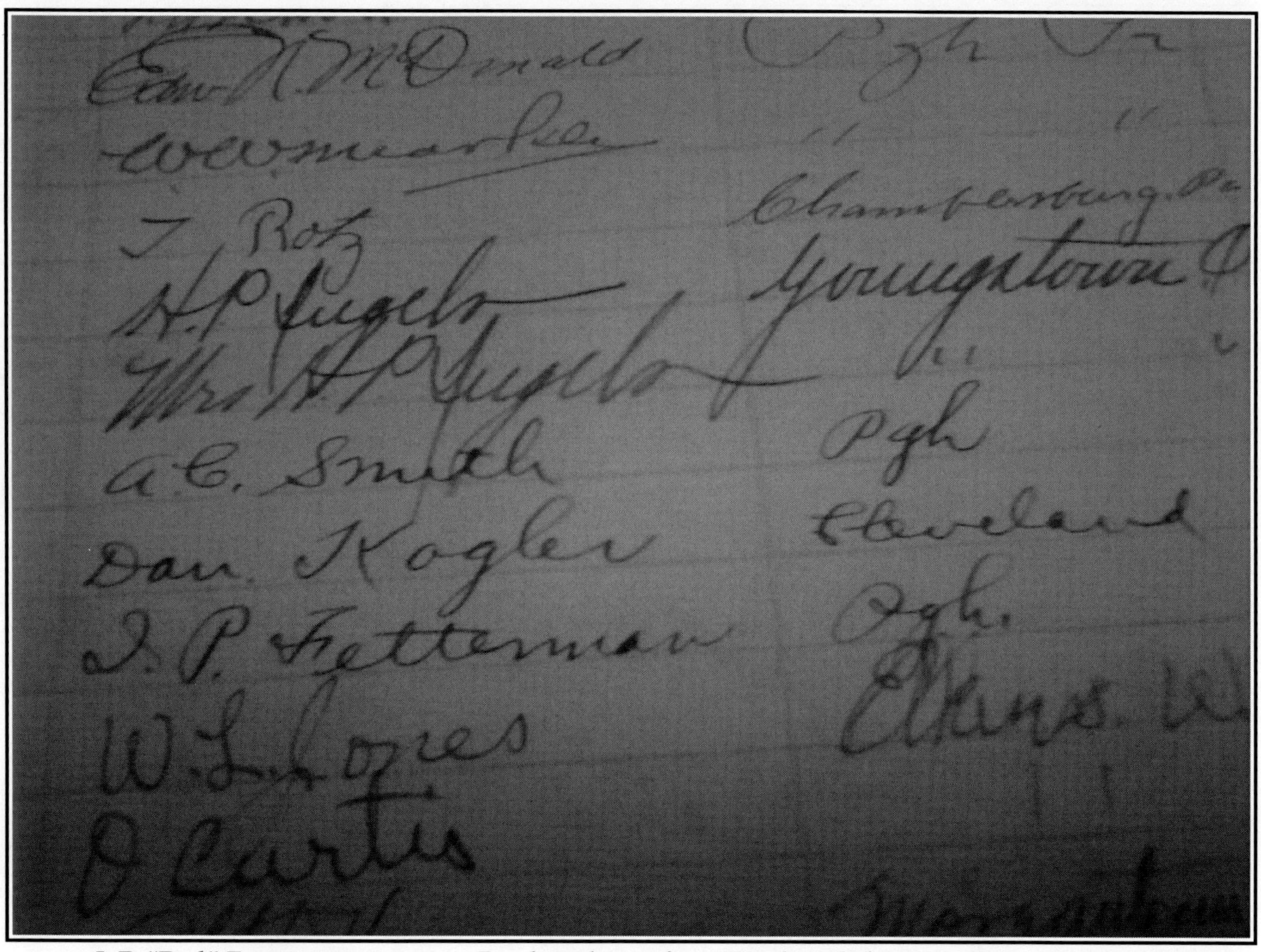

Pgh Pa
T. Rotz — Chambersburg Pa
Youngstown O
A. C. Smith — Pgh
Dan Kogler — Cleveland
I. P. Fetterman — Pgh.
W. L. Jones — Elkins
O Curtis

I. P. "Red" Fetterman was a top Peerless driver from Pittsburgh for F. D. Saup. National backers were making him offers at the last race in 1922.

In July 2014, I wrote a column about long time Titlow bartender, Betty. Here she is...

Betty and the Titlow

Betty Rogers Karwatske is a Uniontown native who is celebrating her 30th work anniversary at the Titlow Tavern & Grille this year. At the age of 18 she waited tables for Charlie May, but she was already familiar with the historic hotel. When Betty was 16 years old her parents went through a divorce. "Mom wanted to work. She was going by the Titlow one day and stopped in. She knew nothing about bar tending. Charlie May and Mom hit it off and he gave her a job. That was in the early 1970's. She was here at least 25 years." It was a great hire.

Charlie gave them a suite overlooking Main Street where they resided for a year and a half. Betty remembers, "I could never sleep there. I had nightmares. Mom always said that there was nothing in the room, but I would hear knocking on the door when there was nobody there. People would be walking around and talking on the balcony, but I could not see them. I practically lived at my friends house because I couldn't be in that room. I always had an awful feeling there was someone watching me. One day around 4 o'clock in the afternoon I was watching TV. I could see something out of the corner of my eye but didn't want to look. I finally turned and saw a hand on the closet door, opening it. It was all wrinkled up. It looked like a woman's hand. I couldn't get out of there fast enough.

"I left the doors open, ran downstairs, and told my mother, 'That's it, I am out of here.' "A lot of people believe and some don't. But it was broad daylight. I stayed at my friends house until we got an apartment."

In 1920, Maude Powell, internationally famous violinist, died of a heart attack in that room, preparing for a concert at the Penn Theater. She was 52 years old.

Nonetheless, Betty soon found herself behind the Titlow Hotel bar. "They just kind of stuck me back there," she smiled. "I knew what a vodka and orange juice was, but that was about all. Someone asked for a Jack Daniels and I said, 'What?' I had no idea. I thought I would never get the hang of it. I can't believe I caught onto it," she laughed.

Betty has experienced many an era at the Titlow. The early days of the welfare hotel, the Main Street Deli, Minnie's Main Street Cafe, the Highland House rock and roll days, WDVE Morning Shows and all, and the Titlow Tavern & Grille of today. "Losing Charlie (May) was hard. He was a wonderful person. People still say how much they miss him. Everyday when he came in, no matter if it was raining or snowing or what, he would say, 'It's a beautiful day out there Little Girl, a beautiful day."

Betty is not a drinker, and when I asked her if she loves her career, she said, "Yes, there is always something happening, never a dull moment. There is always someone hilarious. You do have to be patient, be a shrink, a mother, a babysitter, but if you can pay people no mind it is a fun career. You meet a lot of nice people, hear thousands of stories, make good money, and get plenty of exercise. The Mays have been wonderful to me."

Betty did confess that she refused to do her job just once. Jeff needed fresh towels taken to the room where she saw the hand. She tried, but could not go down that hall. "Many people have had experiences here. Alan (Manager) and I both feel someone following right behind us when we walk down the hall from the kitchen at closing time. It makes the hair on the back of your neck stand up. Recently, a young lady saw an old lady sitting at the lobby desk, then she was gone."

Betty is proud of the way Jeff D'Maio has been remodeling the upstairs again. "The apartments are gorgeous. But I will still not go down that hall."

One of Betty's fondest memories through three decades is of Charlie feeding the homeless men who hung out in the old graveyard behind the hotel. "It's not quite the same without him. There is an emptiness. He was something," she smiled.

Charlie May's portrait hangs in the Titlow Grille dining room. Under it is a light that the staff turns off each night. Many say when they turn around, it is on again.

Visit the Titlow Tavern & Grille every day but Sunday at 92 West Main Street in Uniontown, Pennsylvania. www.titlowtavern.net. Call 724 437-6742.

CHAPTER 3

CONNELLSVILLE AREA LEGENDS

Ed Cope, Three Eras of News Photography

Ed Cope was born in the Connellsville State General Hospital, June 26, 1946 and grew up in Pennsville, Bullskin Township. He is a 1964 graduate of Connellsville Joint High School and served in the Pennsylvania National Guard from 1966 to 1971. They were activated for the 1968 Pittsburgh riots in the Hill District. "I have to say we did not know what we were going to encounter down there. It was a little scary. It was either Good Friday or Holy Saturday. The second night they made arrangements for us to sleep in the Civic Arena.

"I joined the *Connellsville Daily Courier* staff in August 1968. I had no experience in news work or photography at all. I did work under Ed Smith in the Circulation Department while in the Guards. I had been working with my dad at Keystone Fireworks in Dunbar when Bob Broderick, a fellow amateur radio operator suggested I apply for the photographer opening at the paper. Ken Bolden was a one man photo department there and he needed help. Ken took me under his wing as he had several others. I was there for a year when he went on vacation and had a fatal heart attack. I had learned some and was able to go out and shoot most assignments on my own, but I wish I would have had another year with him as my mentor. It was pretty much the school of hard knocks then. We worked a lot of hours. We would go out in the middle of the night when the state police called to shoot accidents, fires and crime scenes to provide them with prints. I worked alone for some time then they hired Charlie Rosendale. He was pretty much self taught, also.

"Charlie and I worked well together and became best friends. We started a photography business in the early 1970's to supplement our incomes. It was called, Edward Cope/Charles Rosendale Photography. We flipped a coin to see whose name went first.

"We did a lot of class reunions, weddings and sports events. We would do up to four weddings each weekend. We shot every kind of sport you can think of, and still worked at the paper. Charlie worked there until 1980 then went to the Uniontown *Herald Standard.* The *Courier* was sold to a Canadian outfit in the mid 1970's and things changed. I went to the *Daily Sunday Tribune* in Monroeville in August of 1981 and worked under Warren Leader, who had I worked with at the *Courier.* They sent me out on assignment to cover the opening of the Parkway East. I figured I would ride down by Channel 4. I wanted to show the traffic in the shot so I got up on this bridge abutment. I had my camera bag on my shoulder and was leaning over. I lost my balance on the bridge and fell. I could have ended up on Ardmore Boulevard. Fortunately for me a tree broke my fall and I landed in a grassy area. All my stuff landed on the ground, too, but I ran a twig up in my eye and thought I lost it. That was one of my nine lives. I drove back to the office with a handkerchief over my eye. It was 90 degrees. They took me to the hospital where they pulled the twig out. Another 1/16th of an inch and I would have been without an eye. We were laid off the day before Thanksgiving the next year.

"I started shooting weddings again and Charlie Rosendale sent me some assignments from Uniontown. In 1983, the *Fay West Tribune Review* Sunday Section hired me as a photojournalist. I worked there until 2003. I had started writing stories a bit at the *Courier.* Bob Broderick was my boss at the *Fay West Tribune Review.*

Photo © Tribune Review

"It was here that I took my award winning shot, "Fire Escape" (above). It is the most cherished picture of my whole career. They were carrying a woman out of a burning building down by Zachariah Connell School in Connellsville. It turned out that it was Sally Driscol, sister of my previous boss at the *Courier.* That picture was chosen as one of the top 600 photos of the century by the Associated Press in 2000. I felt awfully good about that. I was at the right place at the right time to capture the image. I am blessed. I had a one man show and featured it at the Uniontown Law Library. I did a presentation at West Virginia University for Dr. George Esper. I was honored, as a guy with no college education, to speak to college students and show them my work. Esper had been in Vietnam for the fall of Saigon. He was a very interesting man.

"I have photographed people like B Smith in Everson when she first started out, President Carter, Vice President Bush before he became President, governors, people of all walks of life, and ordinary people.

Young B Smith, Everson, PA, mid 1980's. © *Tribune Review*

"Charlie Rosendale and I covered every major news happening in Connellsville, Mt. Pleasant and Scottdale when we worked for the *Courier.* In the year 2003, I became a photographer at the *Herald Standard* under Charlie. When he became ill, around 2008, I took over the job as Chief Photographer until February 2011.

Today, Ed and wife Sue spend winters in Florida. You can find his shots of rocket launches and sun rises on Facebook. Ed's power point presentation shows the gambit of technology he has been through. From the black and white 2 ¼ by 2 ¼ flex camera, to the 35 mm, to digital photography. He taught himself dark room techniques through the years and took several photography and writing classes to learn his craft.

"Life is a learning experience. We yearn to learn. I started out on typewriters, and even learned to lay out pages. As those transitions are happening you have a little fear in you that you won't be able to do it, but you keep going. The digital photography is the best thing that has happened to photographers. We are no longer breathing in chemicals. I feel very blessed to have had a 40 year or so career as a photojournalist without a formal college education."

Ed and Sue dated in the 1970's, then in 1991 got back together and married in 1997. They worked together at the *Herald Standard*. Today, they also take a few digital photos of their grandchildren. Beats middle of the night fires! Ed is also the proud owner of a 1949 Buick Roadmaster, a National Buick Curb winner. "Mom is 94 years old and lives at home. We take care of her. It has been a great ride."

More Ed Cope photographs...Left: Brother Joe, Tent Revival, Mid 1980's. Right: Jimmy Betters plays taps for the Molinara Band, Connellsville, PA *Both photos © Tribune Review*

Heading Home in Springs, PA. © *Herald Standard*

Harold Betters, Christian W. Klay Winery, 2014

Connellsville's Sliding Trombone phenomenon, Harold Betters, continues to play today at age 87...and he can dance...

The Rebirth of Connellsville

In 1906, downtown Connellsville looked like this. Thousands filled the streets for the Centennial celebration. Here, Frick's Coal Arch stands proud, announcing to the world the wealth and prosperity coke and coal had brought to the region. Years later, the downtown became dilapidated. Today, a few good men and women are working hard to build a town to be proud of once again.

Kudos must go out to Michael Edwards, Executive Director of the Downtown Redevelopment Authority, for the immense efforts he and his comrades have put forth to rebuild Connellsville. He may not be a local, but he is fast becoming a legend. Without his foresight, where would Connellsville be? Today, the downtown has new businesses, the Carnegie Free Library has a new roof, playgrounds and streets are fast becoming appealing rather than an eyesore. The list goes on and Connellsville is growing due to his leadership and strength of character. As a past resident of the town, I thank him.

The coal boom is their past, the bike trail, their present and future. Congratulations are due here in a big way. Thank you Michael, and all who support him in the endeavor to pull Connellsville out of the proverbial gutter. More on Connellsville in my upcoming book, *Laurel Highland Legends,* Volume II.

Connellsville Loses Nancy Crislip Henry

Nancy Lizabeth Crislip Henry was born on February 23, 1954, in Connellsville, She was the daughter of Jack E. Crislip, Sr. and Audrey Cavanaugh Crislip. Nancy graduated from Connellsville Area Senior High School in 1972. She then attended West Virginia University, Morgantown, W.Va. and graduated from the Perley Isaac Reed School of Journalism with a Bachelor of Science degree in 1976. Just out of college, Nancy started her career at the former Greengate Mall, Greensburg, Pa. She then went on to work for the *Connellsville Daily Courier* for many years, first as an advertising sales manager and then as a freelance journalist. Her weekly column in the *Daily Courier*, "Around Town" that focused on upcoming events in the Connellsville area was extremely popular with the newspaper's readers. Writing this column was just one of the many ways that Nancy served and supported the community. In addition, she was active in many civic organizations, including Friends of the Carnegie Library, Connellsville Rotary Club, Greater Connellsville Chamber of Commerce, Downtown Connellsville, and Fayette Cultural Trust, where she assisted with *Crossroads* magazine.

The Greater Connellsville Chamber of Commerce recognized her years of dedicated community service and awarded her with the Athena Award. According to the Athena International website, the award honors women or men for professional excellence, community service and for actively assisting women in their attainment of professional excellence and leadership skills. The Athena Award was a fitting award for Nancy, indeed. A Connellsville area resident most of her life, Nancy attended the Connellsville Presbyterian Church.

Nancy died suddenly on August 27, 2015 at the age of 61 at her home in South Connellsville. In addition to her mother, Nancy was survived by her brother, Jack Crislip and his wife, Patty; and her sisters, Marilee McFadden and her husband, Gene, and Kathe Crislip. She was also survived by her nieces, Audra McFadden and Elle Crislip; and her nephew, Michael McFadden. (This tribute was contributed by Susan McCarthy.)

CHAPTER 4

LEGENDS in the MAKING

Skip Seaton, Antique Car Restorer

Skip Seaton of New Salem, Pennsylvania worked for United States Steel in Maple Creek for 20 years. He was as a foreman in the mine for 16 of those, until 1991.

"I always liked cars. When I was a small child I stood up behind the front seat. My dad and I would play a game, name the cars, and I could name them all. Dad liked cars and I had an uncle in the mountains, John King. His son, Ernie, used to come to the family reunions in the late 1950's and take all the little kids for a ride in his Model T. I always told Ernie that he is the one who gave me the disease. It started out in 1965. We bought a 1929 Essex, which is sitting over there," he pointed. "It was our neighbor's car. They were the original owners. If I was not in the yard playing, I was up at the garage looking through the knotholes at that car."

When Mr. King died, the estate sold it to them for $25.00. They had to haul it home. "Ten years later, we had it on the road," Skip laughed out loud. "It would run, but it rotted and needed a lot of work. It was in our wedding in 1975. I bought my first Model T in 1973, a 1923 Roadster. It was like my grandfather's first car. He taught me to drive it. I was 21."

Skip drove the Model T for 20 years, but sold it because he could no longer fit his family in it. "It was one of the fastest Model T's around. Gregg Dahl has it. In 1995, I started Skip's Restoration to restore professionally," he explained, leaning back in his office chair. We were surrounded by vintage cars. Skip spends most of his time maintaining the collections of others. With 20 years under his belt, he has built up an impressive clientele. "Dad always wanted me to go into the restoration business. He died in 1995. I opened the business in the garage he and I started together. The first cars I restored were a Thunderbird and a 1958 Cadillac Eldorado Bridge Convertible. I never looked back."

Today, Skip's collection includes a 1914 Model A he has owned for 41 years, a 1915 Apperson Jack Rabbit, a 1930 and a 1932 Nash, a 1938 Studebaker, a 1950 Studebaker Land Cruiser, and a 1959 Ford. "I used to buy a car a month when I was single and working in the mines," he smiled. "I have been very fortunate to be able to increase and maintain the collection. I have in excess of 20 cars right now. The oldest is the 1914.

"Some of them I have never driven, like the 1966 Volvo. Remember the movie, 'The Saint'? That's the kind of car he drove. It is the P1800. I don't have time to fix it. It came out of a museum setting and sat for a long time. I had it started one time. It came out of Pechins.

"I got married in 1976 and we have three kids. We have always been active in the car clubs. In 1991 we started doing a lot of serious touring because all of a sudden, I had some free time. We've been on 15 Glidden Tours all over the country with our antique cars. We have been as far west as Tuscon, Arizona and Rapid City, North Dakota. As far north as Maine, and as far south as Florida. It was a family deal. The kids would go. My two oldest have awards for being the youngest drivers on tours. This year we have been on three week-long tours in the Model T. We went to Morgantown, Pennsylvania, in June we took it to Heath, Ohio and in July we went to Branson, Missouri. There were 125 Model T's in Morgantown, 30 in Ohio and in Branson, the newest car was a 1916. It was all brass. There were 65 cars there.

"We moved into the Kaufman Motors building here in 2006 which tripled our size. It was also a grocery store before we bought it. Julie does some of the paper work and all the banking and helps when we need her. She drives anything I have, but can't get the hang of the Model T yet."

Most customers come from word of mouth. "I have a web site but haven't updated it for years. Basically, I have been active in the business for 42 years, and people hear about me. There are not a lot of people who do what we do. I am very fortunate to maintain three collections. One guy, I return a car and bring another one back. It is continuous work. We make house calls some times because it is easier. One customer has three Packards. It is better for me to go there to work on them than to transport them. There are eight to ten projects here all the time."

Skip is a life member of the Antique Automobile Club of America and the Studebaker Driver's Club. He belongs to the Horseless Carriage Club, the Veteran Motor Car Club of America, the Model T Ford Club International, the Nash Car Club of America, the Model T Ford Club of America, the Model A Restorer's Club, and the Hudson-Essex Terrapain Club.

"Most of the people I take care of run their cars as much as they can. Some of the bigger, more expensive cars don't get out as much as they used to. I am a big believer in not having trailer queens. Kids come in this shop and I let them get in, blow the horns, show them how to put the roofs up and down. If you don't let the young people touch and feel the cars, and give them experience, the hobby is going to die. You have to let kids understand these are objects to be used. I raised my children in them and I am raising my grandchildren in them. We took all three grandchildren on a tour the other day in the Model A that was our wedding car. Kody started going when he was two. I took him to Daytona on a Glidden Tour. His mother drove the 32 Nash around the speedway there. That is why Julie went. She drove the Apperson in South Dakota and Kentucky. We have made it a family thing and as far as I am concerned, that is what it is supposed to be. Some of the tours cater to the kids. We have auctions with lots of stuff for the kids to bid on. We have made a lot of friends all over the country. I don't think there is a state I can go to where I would not have a friend. I will do it as long as I am healthy enough. Dad finally went on a Glidden Tour with me in 1991. He said that we should have been doing that 20 years ago. We have gotten awards for the biggest family on the tour after that.

"You can get into a Model T for $10,000. to $12,000. You will see younger families with kids in these. There were 35 kids at the tour in Boone, North Carolina. The Model T Club International has a youth editor in their magazine, usually it is a young kid. They are promoting the hobby to kids better than anyone.

"The 1934 Lincoln over there will be going home after I test drive it this weekend, and that 1970 Chevelle will be leaving here in about 15 minutes," he smiled. As we looked over some photographs, the owners of the Chevelle arrived. After a chat with them, I looked around, sat in a Packard, and headed home. I am always smiling when I leave there. It must be the old car disease he mentioned. Skip's restoration is located on Main Street in New Salem, 724 245-2949.

Vintage car tours are a family outing with Skip Seaton of New Salem.

From Barge to Engineer, and a Little Racing

As kids in North Union Township, the Over boys gathered up discarded wood from an old Hopwood bridge that had been torn down. Throughout their boyhood, they built many buildings and bridges, taking one down to build the next. "You had to enter the first cabin through the open-air 'roof'," John Over laughed. "There were no windows or doors. We didn't want anyone else to get in there. I guess we built maybe twelve cabins in all."

They also constructed a track in the yard to race their bikes. They would pretend to be L.J. Dennis in his Rainbow 7. "When I was 16, Dad got us a go kart. I raced it at Fairmont Speedway on Friday nights until college. Dad had raced at Morgantown Speedway, so we had the bug. There was a bunch of guys from here that went, like Dick Rugh. Then when that started to ease up, I would strap the go kart into the trunk of my car and head to Red Line to race.

" When I graduated high school I took a year off to work on the barges. It was the *Patriot* from the Ohio Barge Line that made me want to go to college," he smiled. "It was 30 days on and 30 days off, not an easy life for an 18 year old. It was the winter of '79. I had only been home a week. The river was froze over and we were out for over 45 days. Instead of heading to Pittsburgh from New Orleans, we had to make a detour to Illinois. I guess that was the trip that sealed my fate to go to school and pursue my dream."

The trip from New Orleans and back prompted Over to enroll at Penn State's Fayette Campus where he studied for one year before heading to the main campus. "I have uncles in California who wanted me to come there and gain residency so I could go to a two-year school, but I am a Fayette County home boy."

Over graduated with a degree in Civil Engineering, specializing in structures in 1984. He worked in Northern Virginia and Charleston, South Carolina, but love and the love of home brought him back to Uniontown. "I was fortunate to have the work experience. I learned a lot real quick about the construction business in areas that were growing rapidly."

In 1999, he went into business with a partner and then out on his own in 2002. When I asked what the K2 stood for in K2 Engineering, he said, "My wife Michelle and I call our daughter Kenzie, and she was born the second month of the year." They started out in the old Gabriel's building on Pittsburgh Street near his K2 offices. "At first it was me, an administrative assistant and a draftsperson. That was August, 2002. By October there were five of us." Thirteen years later he employs 35 people and has opened an office in Belair, Ohio. "We build a lot of roads into sites for the gas and oil industry. And do inspections. Our clients are progressive in safety first.

"We are a multi-service firm providing engineering services to 53 municipalities and three counties. We provide many services for companies like the Gabriel brothers. "It has been steady growth. We try to offer excellent service at fair prices. I don't need a million dollars. I just want to support my family and those of my employees.

"I always liked to see how things worked. We used to play with an old drag line that sat in the middle of the field. It is a real old machine with a huge bucket on it. It was inoperable, and had a lot of cables, but that was where we spent a lot of time."

Over began racing stock cars in 2001. He moved up to Late Models in 2007 and continues in the sport today with a little help from sponsors like Bobby Lake and Garry Sisson. He is just getting over a bad accident and is driving once again. He has no plan to ride on a barge again, but is thankful for the experience that pushed him to follow his dreams.

"High school math and science are critical to be interested in for this career. I was blessed to have some very good teachers at Laurel Highlands who assisted my desire to become an engineer. Mrs. D'Auria, Mr. Fitzpatrick and Mr. Diretsky taught me things that I am still using forty years later." K2 Engineering, 234 Pittsburgh Street, Uniontown, PA, 724 439-3440. www.K2 engineering.net

Speaking of Barges

Before the barges got away on the Monongahela River in Pittsburgh in the winter of 2012, a friend suggested I write about the river barge industry. He has worked in it for many years. I agreed. While living in Palmer, I had the pleasure of watching this working river traffic go up and down the "Mon" every day. When I mention the patch town, people often cock their heads to the side and ask, "Is that in Fayette County?" Many do not realize that we still have a strong maritime barge industry, hauling coal up and down the Monongahela River.

Local residents are becoming more and more aware of the growing gas boom, but in Brownsville, career opportunities abound building and maintaining barges. Waterway businesses are not unfamiliar to me. In addition to Palmer, I have lived in a white water rafting community, sailing, ship and yacht building towns, and a waterman's village. I have written about characters who worked on the Youghiogheny River and Chesapeake Bay, but not the "Mon."

I swam in the "Mon" in Palmer two summers running, although I know this may not be a good idea. Fish jumped along our docks, and recreational boats of all kinds went by in addition to river barges. Power boats, pontoons, house boats, jet skis, fishing skiffs, canoes, department store rafts, I saw it all on the "Mon" in my year and a half there. More than a dozen times a day, you could wave at a barge going by. Oftentimes the tug would be pushing three of them. I have photographs of them in all seasons, even with mounds of coal coated with snow.

Presently, Brownsville Marine Products has their own Weld School to train barge builders for this specialty. They run three shifts, five days a week, to build a 200 x 35 foot barge every other day. That is seeing results from your work! As a creative person, watching the barges go by was magic, soothing, like a quiet train. As the nation's economy struggles to stabilize, it is good to know that our region's resources can keep us afloat (pun, I know). A hundred years ago, Palmer was the busiest coal port in the country.

Today, Rosemary Medved, a Palmer native, is the Palmer Patch Historian. I will be writing about her in Laurel Highland Legends, Volume II. She is a LaCava. The Palmer Patch Union Supply Store that Frick built was recently demolished. Rosemary sports the original sign in her garage, above the historical wood figures she is carving. A coal miner, river boat captain, hunter, and more, depict the days gone by in the patch that was once the busiest coal dock in the world.

Marci, Unblocked

Memoir of a Creative Soul

I dove from Mom into Nurse Miller's arms. Our doctor was on vacation. His back-up, drunk at the country club. It was 9 p. m., Thursday night. I was not waiting around Connellsville Hospital for a couple of golfers. The weekend was upon us. Three days later, my sister was so thrilled to meet her fourth sibling, she rubbed my little arms with chicken pox.

At two weeks old I rested on the front seat of Old Betsy between Mom and Mike as we climbed Springfield Pike to her beloved home, the Ohiopyle House Hotel. I found myself in a plastic seat on top of Nanny's long kitchen table among garden vegetables in large bowls, warm homemade bread, fresh noodles and fried chicken. Is that an orange cookie I smell? Soon, someone carried me a few yards to the Youghiogheny River and sat my infant chair on a rock. It was not Mom, Aunt Maralee, and her friends talking about Grandpa Buck passing three months earlier, or the kids yelling and swimming, that woke this newborn. What was that roar? I sighed, opened my eyes. Wild water rushed by glistening in the July sun. Who needs a doctor?

My closest, brother, Kim, took over. He was my comrade from the beginning, rocking my seat, holding my hand, pushing the carriage, holding my bottle, making me laugh. Once he got me crawling, we were a team. Mom was already five months pregnant on my second birthday. I was potty-trained by that November when the sixth baby, Marta arrived. Our three older siblings went to school. We were virtually independent for several hours each day. Mom had to sleep when the baby slept. We did not. I followed his lead to the creek below our house. We tied string to sticks and baited them with the worms we dug up. Fishing, catching minnows and crayfish (we called them crabs), building dams, hiking, playing in the "Tunnels," were our lives.

Around this time my Godmother and

Godfather moved in two houses down on Johnson Lane. Each Wednesday she took me to Ohiopyle to visit her Mom, my Aunt Sade Burnworth. Each Wednesday, she had to pull over just before we got there so I could vomit. She smoked in her new 1955 Chevrolet. Nauseated me even then.

A few years before she passed away she asked me, "Do you remember me taking you to bars when you were a baby?"

"What?" I was shocked. We were not even allowed in the tavern at the Ohiopyle Hotel. We did sneak, of course, but not when we were TODDLERS.

"Yes, I would sit you on the bar. Men love babies. That is how I met Bob" (her second husband).

It came back to me, as they say in the movies.

"I was bait," I said, sickened.

She laughed.

I loved them and thought we were close. Sitting on the steps at home, I listened to Mom talk to her on the phone back then. This is the only way you could find out what adults were up to in our era. No social media photos of their antics were available. This was a secretive generation. When they said to speak when you are spoken to, they meant it. I did not speak to them much throughout life. I did learn the word divorce through eaves-dropping. My Godfather had been good to me. He had always stopped at our house and took us for short rides up the lane in his milk delivery truck. We would run back home. He knew we watched for him out the door almost daily. Although we would see him go by, he never stopped after they divorced and moved away.

We were very busy at the creek and met our neighbors soon thereafter, the Taylors. They lived on the creek and had a constantly growing family like us. I remember their black and white collie biting me on the hand our first visit there. I was three. He was tired of kids torturing him by then, I assume. I heeded that warning. He was old and replaced by a tan and white collie not long after that. The new King never bit me. We were pals. He met me at the front gate and took me to Susie. They had wiener dogs named Fritzie all our lives, too. These were the dogs of my life. I was never attached to our brother's hunting dogs. They were tied to a box for the most part. I spoke to them and petted them sometimes, but they were far from tame like King and Fritz.

My fourth birthday is the first one I recall. My Dad said, "Ask and you shall receive." I asked for and received a fishing pole. It was one of those toy ones, but it was mine. As soon as the birthday candles were blown out and we all had cake and ice cream, I dug up two worms and walked up the road to the "Tunnels" to sit by the creek alone. It was heaven to me. Our house was noisy. My vivid imagination was developing and I was lucky to have a peaceful place to enjoy it. I sat, baited the hook, and cast, a completely happy girl.

Johnson School sat directly across the street from our one and a half story home. My brother and comrade went there a year before me. One morning he smiled his ornery grin and whispered in my ear, "Meet me behind the school at recess." I did.

We ran up Dry Hill and cut back to the creek, playing there the rest of the day. No one ever mentioned it. Imagine that happening today. We were so lucky to be free.

Mom sat me down one day before I headed to Kindergarten. She wrote my name on a piece of paper and pushed it toward me with the pencil. "You need to learn to write your name for school."

I wrote it quick and I remember her head snapping back in surprise. I pushed it back to her and with one leg already out of the red vinyl booth asked, "May I go?" She laughed, nodding up and down.

Besides meeting classmates and making new friends, there are three things that stand out about Kindergarten. I never used the outhouses because of the aroma and wasps. Mom would come get me by the hand and walk me home as if I did not play there everyday of my life on my own. Each day as we stood along Johnson Lane waiting for the coast to be clear before crossing, I'd wonder why she was treating me like a baby. Then I would pull my hand from hers and run across the road and into the yard. Another vivid memory is Mrs. Hixon yelling at me when I went down the sliding board upside down. I thought that she must be a sissy if she thinks that is something and she surprised me because Mom never yelled. I was not used to raised voices that were adults.

After church and Sunday dinner each week, we went to Ohiopyle to visit Nanny, my uncles and cousins, and many fabulous great aunts. Dad only went for the annual reunion. He was always at the Knights of Columbus, golfing or bowling. Picnics along the Yough, standing in the current, watching men dive from the top of the steel bridge, teenagers swinging from the rope across the water and jumping in, swimming to the falls, sometimes over, were the norm. One day a father threw his four and six year old sons off the bridge yelling, "Swim!" They were saved by a local. I still have yet to hear such a blood-curdling scream in my lifetime as the younger boy let out. I stood there, shivering, wondering why no one was doing anything to the father. I wanted to at least kick him hard in the chin. I hoped someone beat him up or held him under for a while.

Our Marietta reunions were bountiful picnics held on Ferncliff Peninsula. I always dreamed about Aunt Jeanie King's baked beans for days beforehand. When she arrived, I was ready with my plate. As a youngster, one of my clear memories at the Hotel is Uncle Bob putting me up over his head and shaking me, saying that he was going to tie me to the railroad tracks. I was all arms and legs swinging trying to get free. Later, he made it up to me by presenting me with his pilot cap from the war. I never took it off. My mother was furious. She was always trying to curl my straight hair and I would put the flaps down over my ears ruining her fine bobby-pin work. My treasured hat disappeared one day. She never confessed. Sure wish I had that today.

In first grade the teacher had us write about ourselves. Under the heading, "Hobbies," I wrote, "Eating." At home I would eat several pieces of bread after dinner, waiting for everyone to leave so I could finish their plates. Dad was a meat-cutter. I took his, "We eat the best cuts of meat, not every family eats Swiss Steak," etc., speeches to heart. Many of my siblings were very picky eaters. They left entire pork chops on their plates. It was heaven to me.

I wrote my first story in first grade, "The Battle Between the Red Ants and the Black Ants." My brothers and I were always messing around with ants. They were very busy and we were very curious. Ants afforded us thousands of hours of entertainment in our youths. The boys even set a tree on fire trying to get rid of ants. I was not there or surely would have stopped them. This same year I began doing sit-ups, jumping jacks, pull-ups, and toe touches each morning. A farm girl in my class told me that she did them before chores and school and I loved the idea. I was soon lifting weights with my brothers. The first try I held 45 pounds above my head while Kim laughed and jumped around yelling, excited and surprised.

Walking through the door at school and seeing a library for the first time, I could not believe my luck. We were allowed to take books home for free and read them. I read every Bobsy Twin and Nancy Drew mystery, Mark Twain, you name it. It was my great escape. The library itself was new that year as was my classroom. We had restrooms in our room. One day a boy kept teasing me, so I chased him around the room and hit him. During this process, I bumped a table and broke a little dog statue. I remember hiding in the restroom. When Miss Mottle returned from the hallway, she called me out. When I told her what happened, he got in trouble. I always found that if you hit bullies really hard, they want to be your friend.

Mom had her seventh baby that year. It is a good thing I was strong, because she slept in a crib next to me for many moons. If I did not stretch my arm to her crib and hold her hand, she cried. Every so often I would turn over to switch arms because the stretched one ached. I shared a bed with another sister or two, depending on the size of the family as it grew.

Saturday mornings were Catechism time. These were different friends than at Bullskin Township school. Nuns, brothers studying to be a priest, they taught us and we managed to enjoy ourselves despite that it was Saturday morning and our friends were sleeping in. I was a tom boy who had to wear a dress every day. Back then we wore our Sunday dress, white gloves and hats to church. To me, getting to cut loose in Ohiopyle afterward was a gift from God. The hotel was four floors. You walked up steps to a huge wrap-around porch. The doors opened into the lobby with the tavern to the right, the dining rooms to the left and the kitchen straight ahead. Nanny's food was legendary. Travelers, fishermen, hunters, conservationists, botanists, and hikers came year after year. It was a diverse crowd of professionals, outdoors people and mountain locals, in addition to my many relatives. There was always cake, cookies, pie, rolls, and a grand meal ready in that kitchen. Who needs a doctor?

Nanny lived upstairs. It was her sanctum from the hard work and bustle. I loved the smell of her rooms. As kids we searched every nook and cranny of the hotel sooner or later, the more off-limits, the more exciting to discover. A couple of our uncles lived there, too, providing us with much entertainment. When we got the nerve to run into the bar, the men would give us pennies. It was well worth the risk of Mom shaking her head at us. I can't remember her ever hitting me, but others got it on occasion. In general, she had a great sense of humor. We were very lucky.

The IQ Test that Changed my Life

Our third grade teacher asked me to read my story, "The Witch and I," in front of the class in 1963. I acted it out and everyone clapped. The principal called me to his office one day soon afterward. My parents were there. I sat between Mom and my teacher,

Mrs. Swink. Mr. Wingrove wanted to move me to fifth grade due to my high IQ test scores.

"No!" my parents said in unison. I suggested that I could be in fourth grade with my brother, Kim. "NO!" Mom hissed at me. I was so little and did not really know what was up, but being in Kim's class sounded mighty exciting to me. I was just trying to help myself have fun in an odd situation.

Wingrove implemented Plan B and hired two people to teach me public speaking. He then used me as his Master of Ceremonies at school plays and PTA events. I recited the Eugene Fields poem, "Seein' Things" many times on the Bullskin Township Elementary stage. These extra activities did not fit into my parent's schedules and were soon squashed. Luckily, I had a talented, eccentric, brilliant English teacher in fifth and sixth grade. She encouraged me to write and speak. I wrote two boxes of stories. She asked me if she could keep them over the summer to read again. Against my gut, I let her. Mrs. Grasso lost them in a flood and broke my heart. I stopped at her home several times during the next few summers asking if she found them. She would just shake her head. This saddened me for years.

Mom's main objective in life has always been, swimming. We went to great lengths to swim in a hundred different places. The river, creeks, lakes, pools, oceans, Mom will get you there, even if we have to push Ol' Betsy home. We did it many times-the Valiant, too. I wonder today, if we were trespassing on the place we called "Snaky Bend." No one ever told us to leave, and others from the neighborhood swam there, too. Mom drove right down into the corner of a field, parked and toted the picnic basket and lemonade through the woods to the water.

Vacations were a close second on Mom's list. Each weekend she lined up her kids and had us put our week's earnings into a coffee can whose lid was taped on for high security. It sat on our food cupboard year-round. Whether you shined Dad's shoes, had a paper route or flipped burgers, you donated to the vacation fund. This can also doubled as a pool-pass fund later in life when we made more money.

Although my creative endeavors were often shut-down by my parents, I wrote and was happy.

Our neighbors, the Taylors (who we love dearly) had eight kids and we had nine. We played baseball and football in their back field and the Johnson School field, and basketball at our hoop along the road. Hide and seek in the evenings, riding bikes, sled-riding parties, picnics, camp-outs, sleep-overs and birthday parties filled our lives. Susie and I held Muscular Dystrophy carnivals through the Jerry Lewis. We were on the Paul Shannon Show with Joe Negri for that. We went door to door summers collecting for it, too. Funny, but we had no qualms about knocking on doors and asking for money.

It was my twelfth birthday when Dad himself, all smiles, presented me with a red and silver bike of my very own. I was beyond happy. He was so proud. Had bought it used for $15. It was a red beauty. I no longer had to ask people to borrow their bikes. This meant total independence to me.

Both our families had station wagons and rented summer beach houses in Sea Isle City, NJ for two weeks at the same time for many years. Running free on the beach and its little town, and having so much freedom at home as a child, did not prepare me for the need to fight for it during my teens.

Seventh grade is when you mix your

childhood friends with kids from other neighborhoods. I went to the Cameron Building in downtown Connellsville and enjoyed several of the teachers there. One was blind, Mr. Egnot, but the best I think I have ever had in school. It was this year that Dad started putting a lid on my social life. My older sisters were wallflowers, and he had no sisters, so he was not used to a girl asking to go to dances, parties and ice skating. "No," was the answer I got every time. Just getting up the nerve to ask to do anything became nerve-wrackingly stressful. I walked on eggshells around him and spent a lot of time in a certain apple tree. Mom never went against Dad. Her generation was that way, so I stuck to my neighborhood for the most part, a bit confused about why that was necessary when everyone else had other friends .

I was a ninth grade cheerleader who broke her ankle playing football in Taylor's back field. My boyfriend that year was a good basketball player. Mom let me go to friend's houses and play basketball with him. When I finally asked if he and his mother could pick me up before the annual dance, the answer was, "No."

I did not have the nerve to tell him and when they showed up out front, Dad refused to let me go. He took me himself. The humiliation stuck in my throat. I don't think I talked to anyone all evening. Dad picked me up and sat outside Miedel's Restaurant, giving me 15 minutes with my friends after the dance. I was an A student who had never been in trouble. I did not understand why he didn't like me anymore. Now, of course, I know I scared him. He couldn't handle a daughter who was not a follower and did not have the skills to handle me as I drew away from him. Neither did Mom.

I don't know about your house, but in our house no one ever talked about anything of importance. For instance, I had a Mom and two older sisters. No one ever mentioned their period, sex or pregnancy. Mom would not even let me go watch the menstruation movie in fifth or sixth grade. A girl told me black stuff comes out of girls. Although the whole outcast thing was odd, I did not give the film's contents a thought after the days it was shown and I sat with another girl in the classroom while several grades went to the auditorium. When I found myself bleeding I came out of the bathroom and tapped Mom's shoulder as she ran the sweeper. She shoved me back into the bathroom with a huge narrow diaper type object. I had to consult my sisters. She had not said one word about what to do with it. It was a figure it out for yourself kind of world then.

Counting the days until my fifteenth birthday so I could get my work permit, I sent for it, then watched the mail. The day it arrived I gathered my writing samples and courage and walked up the road to the house of the newspaper's Circulation Manager, Mr. Smith. He was home. I shook his hand and told him I would like a chance to work at the *Courier.* He accepted my stories and called me two days later. I was invited on a tour. Mom took me Saturday morning. I was in heaven, finally, a creative outlet I can sink my teeth into! As we stood and talked at the end of the tour, he said I could come in a 10 a. m. Saturdays to begin. Mom burst out laughing. I looked at her, shocked. We thanked him. In the car she informed me that I would work at the Tastee Freeze with my older siblings. End of discussion. Mom and I broke up that day.

Staring a the grill standing next to my oldest sister, she was "training" me to cook and wait on the counter and booths. I was still in shock. My parents would not let me choose my friends or my profession, but being a writer, I wrote about those around me. Here, they happened to be stoned teenagers coming in for burgers. One of my sisters started dating a boy from Giebel, the local Catholic High School. My cousin was friends with them and we were friends with many of them from church. Although they were several years older, Mom and Dad thought it a better idea if I hung with them. They partied, had sex, took me over the state line to get beer, and drove fast cars. I researched, experimented and wrote, but did not speak to my parents much throughout those years.

My Senior High building was brand new my sophomore year. Tenth grade was the first year girls could wear slacks to school. Mini skirts were pissing off the principals, too. High School was a study of pot and poetry. I embroidered my jeans. Life is a carnival, peace, love, roller coasters and rainbows. They also just built a vocational school. It is a bit of a blur, but we had fun. I did everything the opposite of what my parents requested.

On my 16th birthday I was grounded. Dad was on guard sitting in his chair at the window below my bedroom. I remember him coming upstairs to see if I was smoking pot. Of course I was. I jumped out my window and into the bushes as he descended the stairs. I ran up the road and through the woods to the local hang out. Happy Birthday to me.

In my Senior year of high school I took a sociology class at the local college campus where I excelled. It was exciting, but my parents did not understand my complete boredom and need for stimulation. They took me to a psychologist because they were at their wits end living with my silence and anger. I never spoke to the counselor. They took me twice. When they asked why I would not talk to him, I said, "One look at him and you can see he has bigger problems than me."

At this time I was riding around in the evenings with a friend who was a junkie. I do not know or care what people thought, but we listened to great music and smoked pot. I wrote poems that I still have. In his big warm Chevelle, we rode in silence most of the time, humming along to the Rolling Stones. We both needed the pleasant escape from our families.

One day not long before graduation, a friend and I walked to Ohiopyle. I never went home again..

"I believe that a simple and unassuming manner of life is best for everyone, best both for the body and the mind." - Albert Einstein

Author's Bio

Author, historian, storyteller, Marci Lynn McGuinness, has been writing since she was six years old. She started self publishing books and magazines in 1981, and will continue until she falls in the river or drowns in the sea.

McGuinness is blessed with healthy daughters and sons-in-law, a wonderful man and Avie, her grandson of two years.

She is the middle child of nine and has a way of skating around stress to get her books to press. " I often hide for periods of time. It is impossible to create in chaos chasing the dollar. Life should not be based on the love of money or the fear of its absence. Sure, we need it, BUT it is only paper and has nothing to do with real life. Love, eat food that you grow, laugh...and do it again." ---Marci Lynn McGuinness

Books by Marci McGuinness

Laurel Highland Legends, Volume I

Vivian & the Board Track Boys (2015/e book/story)
The Mystery of the Ohiopyle Hotel (2015 e book/story)
Murder in the Vineyard (2014)
Pam's Cooking (with Pam Bendishaw - 2013)
1915 Uniontown "Summit Mountain" Hill Climb Program Reprint
Murder in St. Michaels (4/2013)

Ohiopyle, That Little Town, WWII (Lillian McCahan & McGuinness) (2012)
Speedway Kings of Southwestern Pennsylvania, 100 Years of Racing History (2011)
Yesteryear at the Uniontown Speedway (1996, 2nd Edition 1997, 3rd Edition 2008)
Official Program U.S.A. Speedway, 1916 Reprint (1996, 2nd Edition 2009)
Message of the Sacred Buffalo (June 2010)
Hauntings Of Pittsburgh & the Laurel Highlands (October 2009)
Gone to Ohiopyle (September 2009)
Murder in Ohiopyle & Other Incidents (Summer 2009)
Butch's Smack Your Lips BBQ Cookbook, (Spring 2009)
Yesteryear in Ohiopyle and Surrounding Communities, Volume III (2008)
How to be a Working Author/Writer (2005; 2nd Edition, Fall 2008)
Chesapeake Bay Blue Crabs (2004)
In it to Win It (2001)
The Explorer's Guide to the Youghiogheny River, Ohiopyle and SW PA Villages (2000)
Along the Baltimore & Ohio Railroad, from Cumberland to Uniontown (1998)
Stone House Legends & Lore (1998)
Yesteryear in Smithfield (1996)
Yesteryear in Masontown (1994)
Yesteryear in Ohiopyle and Surrounding Communities, Volume II (1994)
Yesteryear in Ohiopyle and Surrounding Communities, Volume I (1993)
No Outlet! (1993)
Incidents (1992)
Nanny's Kitchen Cookbook (1991)
Natural Remedies, Recipes & Realities (1986)
The Deerhunter's Guide to Success...from the woods to the skillet (1985)
Natural Remedies (1984)
Unforgettable Poems for Everyday People (1984)
What's Happenin' Around Ohiopyle (1981)

More Publications by McGuinness

Around Ohiopyle Map & News July 2009-present (annual)
Around Ohiopyle Magazine (2008)
Tying the Knot Magazine (2007)
St. Michaels/Tilghman Coupon Booklet (2003)
Yesteryear Calendar series (1990's)
Yesteryear Press (Newsprint Magazine-5 times a year) 1992 - 2002
Speak Easy Digest (Early 1990's-quarterly)
Naturally Yours Newsletter (1980's)

Movies/Scripts

Speed Kings screenplay based on Yesteryear at the Uniontown Speedway board track (2010)
Murder in St. Michaels screenplay based on mystery, Murder in St. Michaels (2005)
Yesteryear in Ohiopyle - The Movie (1990's)

www.ohiopyle.info, shorepublications@yahoo.com,
www.amazon.com/author/marcimcguinness

Laurel Highland Legends, Volume II

In the next volume of *Laurel Highland Legends,* I will interview as many of the people who provide local products to the Backyard Gardens store on Lincoln Street (one block from the falls) in Ohiopyle as possible.

Maple Syrup, honey, photographs, wooden toys, painters, soap-makers, jelly and butter makers, bakers, crafts people and farmers will be included. I hope to interview Art McGann, WWII veteran of Connellsville, an old coal miners or two, moonshiners, politicians, and who knows who.

There will be opportunities for you to publish a "Family/Clan" page or Legend page of your favorite area legend ($100. per page). Share recipes, remedies, adventures and photos. Contact: shorepublications@yahoo.com.

A big THANKS to the sponsors on the following pages and cover. With their assistance, I bring you *Laurel Highland Legends,* Volume I.

Coming in Laurel Highland Legends, Volume II...

Interviews with Speed Kings and more!

Michael Lake, an Albert Gallatin School student, is now 14 years old. He races a Super Late Model car in several states, beating veteran drivers with a cool, calm disposition. More on this young Laurel Highland phenomenon in *Laurel Highland Legends*, Volume II.

GMS Harley Drag Team Racer, Gregg Dahl, 2015. Sixty feet in 1.309 seconds! Napierville Speedway.

Stacey Bortz races in the Outlaw Street class of the AMRA and she is the first woman in the world to make an 8 second quarter mile pass on a Street (no wheelie bar) Harley Davidson.

More on these Speed Kings in *Laurel Highland Legends*, Volume II!

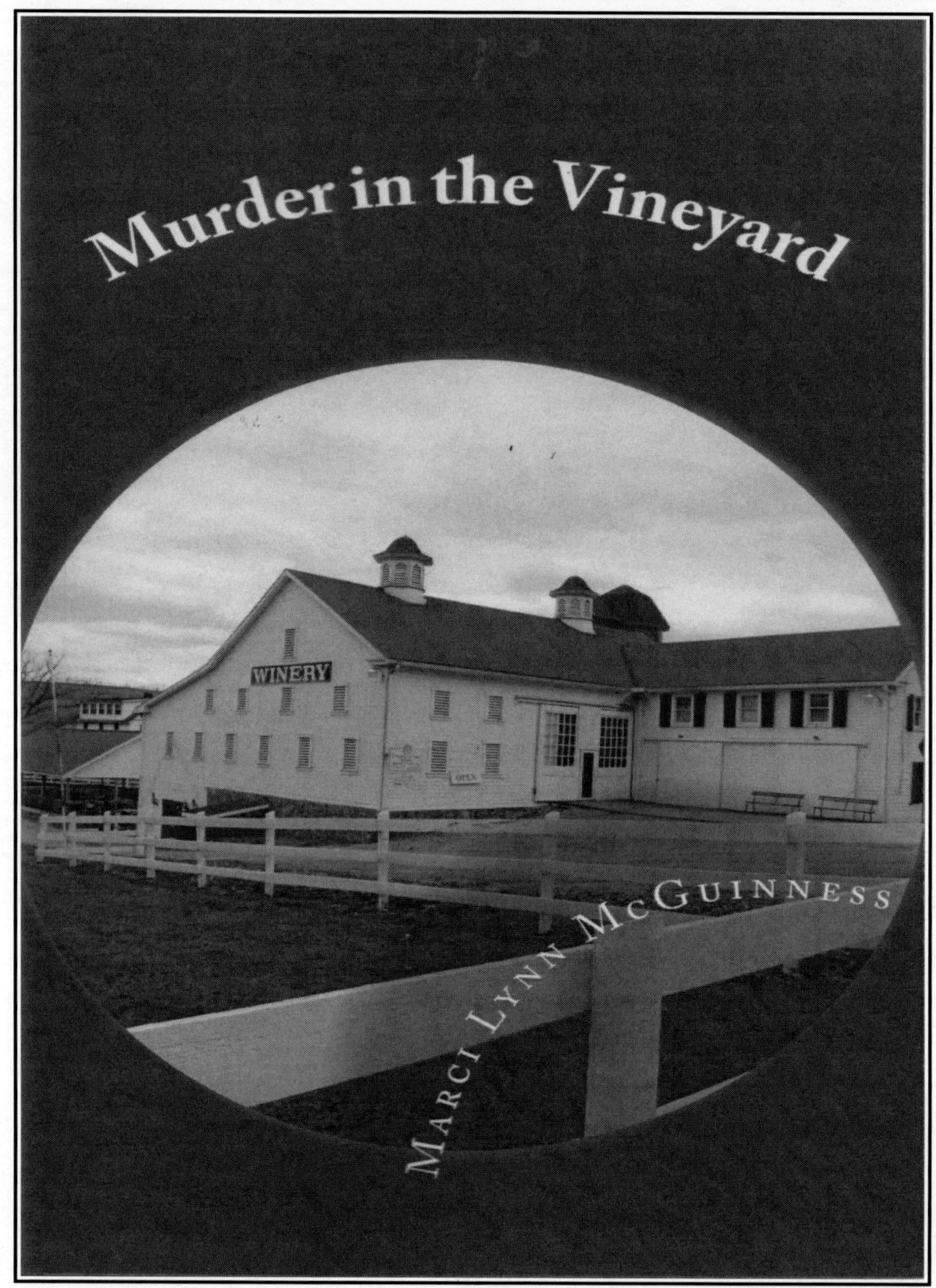

Why is the Senator still haunting the Christian W. Klay Winery in Chalk Hill, PA? Find out in McGuinness' historical novella, *Murder in the Vineyard*.

A Must-Read Children's Book

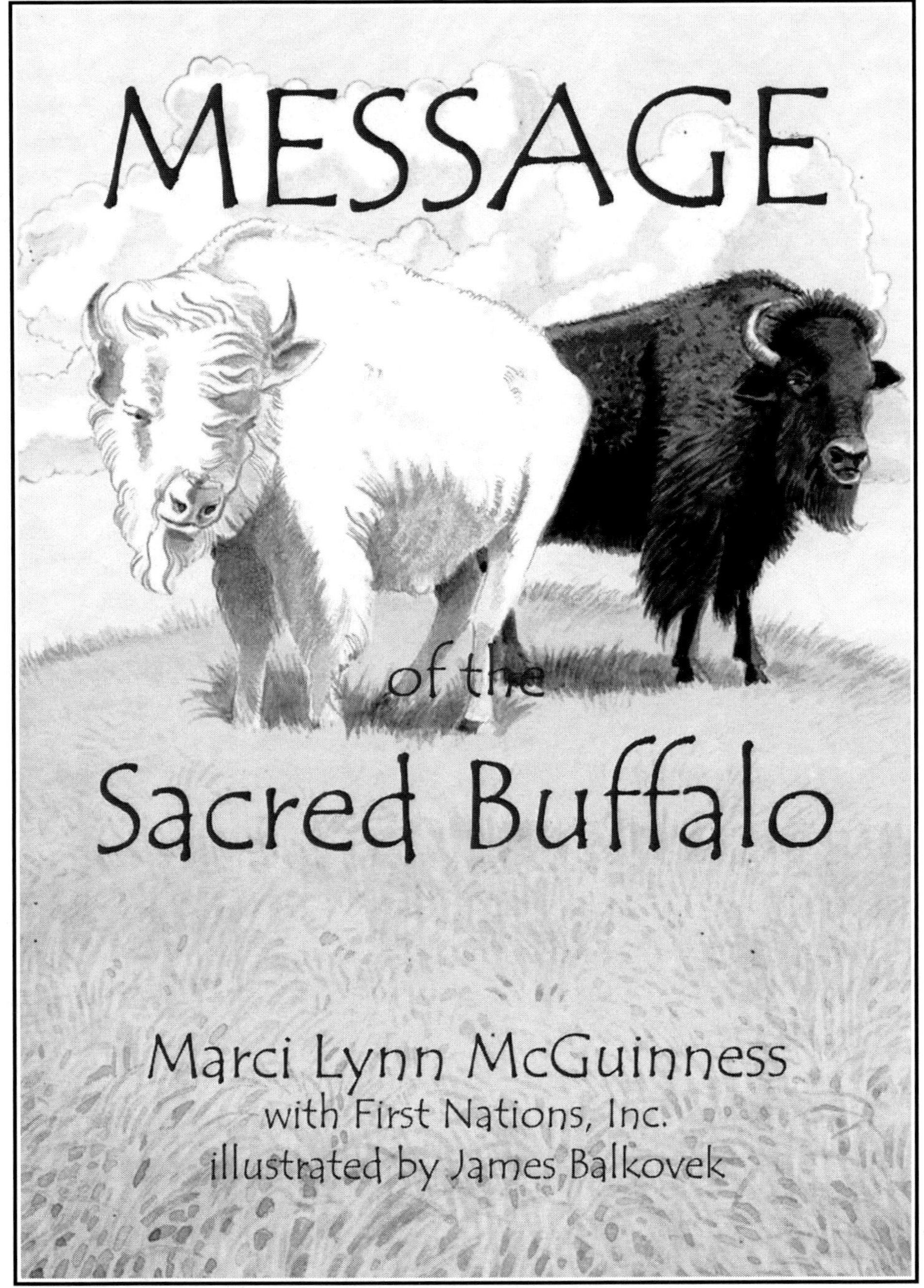

Who are the Sacred Buffalo of Farmington, Pennsylvania and why are they here? Discover their message in this beautiful historical legend.

Join the author on paranormal visits to historical Laurel Highland gems like the Titlow Tavern and Grille where someone asked, "Where's Marci?!" On a journey to the West Overton Museum in Scottdale, an orb traveled down McGuinness' leg. It came out of the attic in the new gift shop there. Find out what happened to her next in this real life ghostly battle that led her to the Sacred Buffalo of Farmington.

A few years ago, Ross Rogalski sent me a box of manuscripts and letters that had belonged to Lillian McCahan. In it were letters from dozens of Ohiopyle area soldiers fighting in World War II. From many countries, they wrote of their whereabouts and what was happening to them. In *Ohiopyle, That Little Town, WWII,* I publish many of those letters in addition to photographs and input from soldiers who are still with us.

Watch for McGuinness' next book... *Laurel Highland Legends*, Volume II.

For Interviews with...

Art McGann, Connellsville WWII veteran
Cheryl Whipkey, Ohiopyle native who was in the Ohiopylle Hotel on November, Friday the 13th when an arsonist set it ablaze in 1964
Rosemary Medvec, Palmer Coal Patch Native and Historian
Ronnie King, Retired Coal Miner
Hap Crawford, Mortician Extraordinaire
Gregg Dahl and Stacie Bortz, Legendary Harley Drag Racers setting world records
Dave Dahl, decades as a square dance Disc Jockey
Fred Zeigler, Twenty Years at the Stone House Inn
Pete Hook, Country Lawyer
AND...
Marci, Unblocked, Part II (Memoir)
More histories, mysteries and photographs from Marci McGuinness
Ohiopyle Reunion photographs, identified
Guseman Family Race Track photographs
Ohiopyle Shop Owner Interviews
Local artists, wood worker and creative folks interviews
Wine and Whiskey in Chalk Hill
AND much more.

Be a part of *Laurel Highland Legends*, Volume II

Include your family history page, photographs, a story about a local legend, an ad for your business or organization, and/or a cover photograph. Contact the author at: shorepublications@yahoo.com or 304 698-6207. Information is also available at: www.ohiopyle.info.

Find All of McGuinness' Books on Amazon and Kindle.

Find them locally at Backyard Gardens in Ohiopyle and Pechin Supermarket in Dunbar (PA).

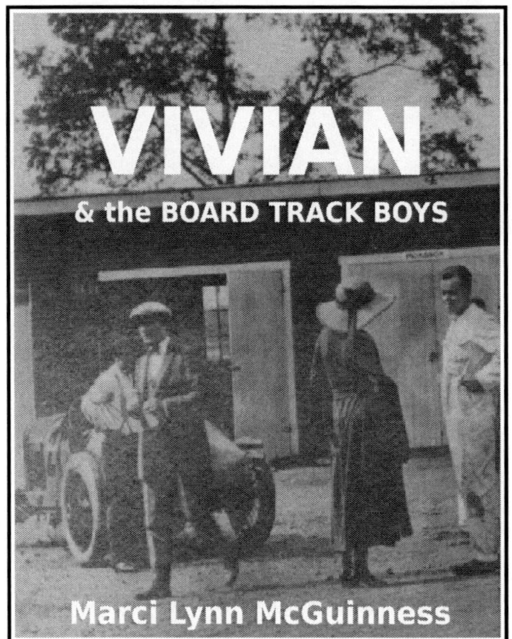

Enjoy McGuinness' original historical fiction inside this first volume of *Laurel Highland Legends.*

More on Marci Lynn McGuinness at:

www.ohiopyle.info

Made in United States
Cleveland, OH
14 November 2024